A Basic Guide to Cheese

Pascale Maby

A Basic Guide to Cheese
Pascale Maby

Holt, Rinehart and Winston of Canada, Limited

Toronto   Montreal

HOLT, RINEHART AND WINSTON OF CANADA, LIMITED
55 HORNER AVENUE
TORONTO

COPYRIGHT
© 1973, HOLT RINEHART AND WINSTON OF CANADA, LIMITED

© 1972, LES ÉDITIONS LA PRESSE

COVER AND INTERIOR COLOUR PHOTOGRAPHS
COURTESY OF BARIBOCRAFT

LIBRARY OF CONGRESS CATALOG CARD NUMBER: 73-3884

ISBN : 0-03-929926-0

PRINTED IN CANADA

1 2 3 4 5   77 76 75 74 73

Table of contents

Introduction

According to the Bible, (2 Samuel, XVII, 29), King David and his starving people, after crossing the desert, arrived in Manahaim, where they were given a meal which contained, amongst other things, cream and cow's milk cheese. Cheese is as old as civilization itself. There is one sculptured in the stone of a 6,000 year old Chaldean bas-relief from the city of Ur. It was known to the Greeks, the Assyrians, and the Egyptians. Homer mentions it in the Odyssey, as does Virgil in his Georgics ; and Aristotle, putting philosophy to one side for a moment, explains how it is made. Let us think back for a moment to our prehistoric ancestor who first had the curiosity to milk a cow or a sheep. In this accidental gesture we find the humble beginnings of all the Camemberts, Gruyères, Roqueforts, Gorgonzolas, and other delicacies that future generations were to derive for our benefit.

If we travel down through the centuries, and pick out some of the more famous cheese lovers on our way, we end up with names such as Attila the Hun, Charlemagne, Louis XI, the poet Charles of Orléans, Rabelais, Henry IV '' le Vert Galant '', the no less gallant Louis XIV, Louis XV, Casanova and Napoleon Bonaparte, Prince Metternich, and Talleyrand — prince, diplomat, statesman, and famous extoller of the qualities of Brie...

However, in spite of these examples, it was not until the middle of the 19th century that cheese finally gained its place of honor in fine dining. Looked down upon by gourmets, considered in fact as vulgar peasant food, it had to overcome a great many prejudices before being proclaimed the '' king of desserts ''. Naturally, its champion was a Frenchman. Anthelme Brillat-Savarin (1755-1826), gastronome and author of '' The Physiology of Taste '', stated that '' the most marvellous menu was nothing more than heresy if it did not contain (any) cheese, if only to increase one's appreciation of the wines. '' From this point on, its reputation bolstered by snobbishness, cheese made its solemn entry into all the so-called " finer " meals, but it was a while yet before it gained a place in dining rooms where the whims of fashion counted for little.

In effect, though of ancient lineage, it is only in the last hundred years or so that cheese has come into common use. Celebrated by poets and all those with discriminating palates, it is now recognized as one of the tastiest of foods, and, in addition, one of the most energy-producing. But how many of us know what it is made from or how ? This is what we will now look into briefly, bearing in mind however that this is not a technical book, but simply an initiation into the elementary principles of cheese-making.

Ah ! there, madame, a good cheese !
Ah ! there is a good milk cheese !
It comes from the country of him who made it.
He who made it, it is from his village...

(17th century Norman song)

Part one

ALL ABOUT CHEESE

*Cheese is the finest
of all desserts.*

Talleyrand-Périgord (1754-1838)

How Cheese is Made

It is easy to imagine that the first cheese must have come into being accidentally, much to the amazement of that prehistoric ancestor we mentioned earlier. Probably having forgotten that he had put some of his precious supply of milk aside for safekeeping, imagine his surprise at seeing his milk transformed into curds. Many great discoveries are the result of absent – mindedness! Having become a cheese-maker in spite of himself, we can again imagine him tasting his product, declaring himself satisfied, and passing the secret on to his descendants...

The earliest Canadian cheese-makers were French colonists who, at the beginning of the 18th century, began producing milk products according to the ancestral methods of their native provinces (Normandy, Brie, etc.). Later, the United Empire Loyalists introduced typically British recipes. These small, regional centers of production slowly gave birth to a vast industry that has not stopped growing since 1864, the year in which the first cheese factory in Canada was built.

Since then, the creation of new, essentially Canadian types of cheese and the technical contributions of immigrants from several different countries, each with their own characteristic processes, have helped to increase the range of products offered. Today there are about thirty main types, whether Canadian or foreign in origin. The range of the latter proves to be very cosmopolitan. It is even possible to obtain, made in Canada, the famous Greek Feta, so popular in its own country.

Some steps in the making of cheese at the Abbey of St. Benoit du Lac (Quebec)

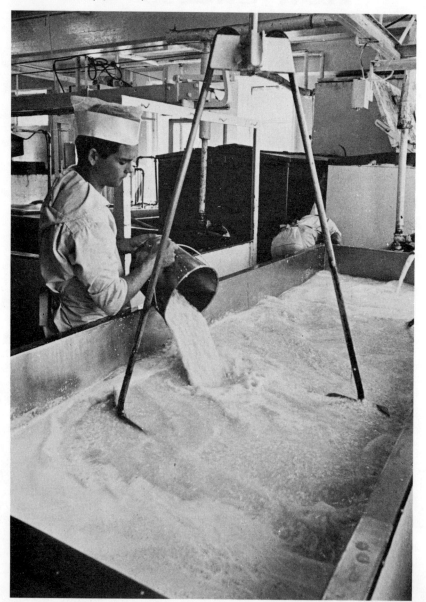

A careful blend...

Smoothing the paste

Forming

The settling

Turning the cheese out of the mold and powdering the skin.

Every cheese factory is frequently inspected by both the Federal and Provincial Health Departments. The provincial inspectors are responsible for checking the milk used in the manufacturing of the cheese, and the federal government controls the classification of the finished product, the fat content and the degree of moisture. Furthermore, federal inspectors visit all retail outlets regularly to check the quality and the state of the cheeses offered to the consumer.

" Cheddar is made from whole milk. A special bacterial culture which produces lactic acid is added to the milk. The mixture is stirred and heated in vats to 86°F., then coloring is added as well as curdling agents, such as rennin. The resulting curd is cut into one-quarter inch cubes which are again stirred and heated. Once the curd is firm, it is drained. The curd is left to settle and then is cut into small pieces the size of buns which are turned over from time to time. The smooth curd is cut into thin strips, salted, then compressed into blocks or wheels.

After being taken out of the press, each block or wheel is stamped with the date, the batch number, and the vat number. Cheeses destined for export are also stamped ' Canada '. The cheese is then wrapped or paraffined to prevent weight loss and mould. Then it is aged in temperature-controlled warehouses. The aging process, of different lengths of time and at different temperatures, gives the desired flavour. "

(Canadian Department of Agriculture)

Low Fat Content Curd

When milk is left to stand in a closed receptacle at a normal temperature, it decomposes into lactoserum (whey) and cream, which, since it is lighter, rises to the surface. The milk is then brought into contact with the air, and the casein coagulates, separates from the cream, and settles to the bottom in the form of curd. This, which is not at all creamy, will give a cheese which is low in fat content.

High Fat Content Curd

On the other hand, if this same milk is left exposed to the air right from the beginning at a temperature of about 77°F., the coagulation of the cream is accelerated and precedes the decomposition into cream and lactoserum. The curd remains combined with the cream and is used to produce a high fat content cheese.

Naturally, bearing in mind the amount of time that is necessary for the complete separation of the milk into creamy curd and lactoserum, it is possible to control the richness of the resulting curd. The percentage of fat content is determined by allowing more or less time for the elimination of the lactoserum.

Rennin

On the industrial scale, in addition to a heating process, the curdling of the milk is speeded up by adding rennin, an extract from the stomach of certain young ruminants (calves, lambs, and kids). The precise amount, carefully calculated, varies according to the type of cheese in question.

Transformation of the Curd into Paste

The curd, drained, but still very moist, can already be eaten as a fresh cheese, as is or after adding cream, salt, or sugar to reduce its acidity (cream cheese, Petit-Suisse). It can also be used to make a soft-ripened cheese (Camembert, Livarot, Munster, etc.).

Drained for a longer period of time, worked, kneaded, sometimes heated and even pressed to eliminate more lactoserum, the curd which is now firmer will produce a semi-soft or a hard cheese (Saint-Paulin or Gruyère type).

Moulding or Shaping

Once the desired consistency is achieved (soft or hard), the

19

pasty curd is then placed in moulds where the cheese takes on its eventual shape. The inventiveness of cheese-makers has produced moulds in every shape imaginable (wheel, square, brick, pyramid, ball, sausage, pear, etc.) and some shapes are used to identify certain types of cheese.

Salting

Once moulded, the paste is salted. It is simply sprinkled with salt in the case of a downy-crusted cheese (Brie, Camembert) or dipped in a brine solution in the case of a cheese with a washed crust (Livarot, Munster). All semi-soft or hard cheeses are salted in brine.

Not only is salting very important to the future flavor of the cheese, but it also speeds up fermentation and the formation of the crust.

Fermentation

Lactoserum contains several fermenting agents. A cheese which retains a large quantity of it at the curdling stage ferments more easily. This is the case with soft cheeses which quickly develop mould on the outside (penicillium) and thus downy crusts which are then cleaned on certain types. At the same time, the flavor and the aroma are developed, more or less strong, depending on the amount of fermentation. A soft cheese is almost alive, and never stops fermenting. It must therefore be eaten when all the desirable qualities such as perfume, taste, consistency, and appearance are at their peak. The critical point which must not be passed is when the amino acids of the proteins begin to change into ammonia.

Semi-soft, hard, or extra-hard cheeses, less rich in lactoserum and consequently in fermentation, do not have this inconvenience and will keep longer. They ferment much more slowly, especially if the air has been pressed out of them.

Pasteurization

The pasteurization of cheeses did not begin until 1935. Though this process destroys some of the bacteria which are harmful to the preservation of cheese, it destroys, at the same time, the majority of the elements which contribute to giving it its full flavor. These must then be replaced with other fermenting agents able to produce similar effects ; but the results rarely satisfy a connoisseur, especially as far as soft cheeses are concerned. However, pasteurization has the great advantage of considerably increasing the life span of a cheese without its nutritional qualities being in the least affected.

Chambertin and Roquefort are both excellent foods for refreshing a love, and bringing a budding love to quick maturity.

(Casanova-Memoirs)

Different Types of Cheese

To begin with, the expressions *unwashed, downy mould crust, interior mould* characterize the type of cheese and in no way reflect the hygiene of its manufacturer.

Soft Cheeses

- Soft, kneaded, unfermented. Mild fresh flavor. (Cottage Cheese, Petit-Suisse, Boursin, Provençal, etc.).

Fermented Cheeses

- Soft, unwashed, with a downy mould crust. Very delicate and pronounced flavor. (Brie, Camembert, Coulommiers, etc.).

- Soft, washed, with a mouldless crust (the mould has been scraped off). Flavor more pronounced and less delicate than those already mentioned. (Livarot, Maroilles, Munster, etc.).

- Blue cheese. The interior moulds are due to fungi which are combined with the curds. Strong or extra-strong taste. (Blue, Gorgonzola, Roquefort, Stilton, etc.).

- Semi-soft, pressed, uncooked, or slightly cooked. Mild, nutty flavor. (Gouda, Saint-Paulin, Oka, Limburger, Anfrom, Capucin, etc.).

- Hard, pressed, cooked. After stirring, the paste is cooked for an hour and a half at 140°F. Mild nutty flavor. (Emmenthal, Gruyère, etc.)

- Extra-hard, pressed, cooked. Very strong, spicy taste. (Pecorino Romano, Parmesan, etc.)

Process Cream Cheese

- These are altered cheeses, obtained by melting in a vacuum at 105°F. cheeses of the Gruyère, Roquefort, Emmenthal, and similar types. Very little of the original taste and aroma remain. In some cases the flavor is increased by the addition of various ingredients : cumin, ham, salami, shrimp, vegetables, etc.

In the world today there are more than 500 different types of cheese made from the milk of all kinds of animals . Milk from the cow, goat, sheep, mare, reindeer, yak, llama, and the buffalo are all used.

Fat Content

Since dietetics is a field which is beginning to hold more and more interest for the consumer, it would be helpful if all manufacturers would mark the fat content on their products. When this does appear on the package, one should bear in mind, before worrying about it, that the percentage shown refers to the cheese as ulta-dry. This means that in the case of soft cheeses, which often contain more than 50% water, the true percentage of fat content must be reduced by at least one half. Thus the true fat content of a Camembert when eaten is no more than 25% and an 8-ounce package contains no more than 2 ounces of fatty substances.

In general, the hard cheeses are the richest. Having a greater amount of dry substance, they provide more calcium, phosphorus, and vitamins. Some cheeses are true energy foods (Chester, Emmenthal, Gruyère).

Classification of cheeses according to fat content

(Cheeses considered as ultra-dry)

TYPE :	PERCENTAGE :	EXAMPLES :
Lean	0 to 20%	Cancoillotte, Cream Cheese.
Semi-Fat	20 to 40%	Parmesan, Pecorino, Mozzarella.
Fat	40 to 45%	Anfrom, Edam, Roquefort, Gruyère, Emmenthal.
Extra-Fat	45 to 60%	Blue Cheese, Camembert, Cheddar, Port-Salut, Gouda, Demi-Sel, Colby, Brie.
Double-Cream	over 60%	Petit-Suisse, Suprême.
Triple-Cream	over 75%	Petit-Suisse, Brillat-Savarin, Semrival.

It is practically impossible to make a cheese with a fat content of more than 77%.

The fat content varies from one cheese to another. It is possible to get cheese made from skim milk, which is very low in calories. Dry cottage cheese contains about one quarter the number of calories as an equal amount of Cheddar. Creamed cottage cheese gives about twice as many calories as the natural type.

Full of vitamins and calories, cheese is a gourmet delicacy which does not make one gain weight when used in moderation.

Cheese and the Diet-Conscious

Dietetics is not a new science. The Greeks, who also used cheese as an antidote for poisons, used to give it to athletes who were training for the Olympic games. The Roman legions did not leave to conquer the world without taking an ample, supply of it along in their chariots. Attila and his Huns stoked up their energy and their ferocity with cheese that they made from the milk of their mares. Clovis, King of the Franks, who had a tendency to gorge himself on salt pork and hard boiled eggs, was put on a diet by his doctor which consisted solely of cheese.

Although medicine no longer places full confidence in cheese and even banishes it as soon as certain dietetic restrictions are imposed, it is still considered as a food with a high energy and calorie value which is always profitable to eat in balanced amounts. Very digestible, with the exception perhaps, of a few soft-ripened cheeses with washed crusts which take a bit longer to assimilate, it is the most economical source of all kinds of proteins which are indispensable to the organism. It is recommended for children (especially Gruyère) and adolescents who refuse to drink milk. Its nutritional value is almost identical, its calcium is good for growth and its phosphorus for mental activity. Finally, soft cheeses, particularly those with interior mould, are the richest in vitamin B.

Is Cheese Fattening ?

Though it is a rich food, there is no danger to the waistline if it is eaten in moderation. One should simply bear in mind

that 3½ ounces of cheese (with the exception of the lean cheeses) are on the average equal to about 8 or 9 ounces of meat and represent a minimum of 300 calories.

A precious source of calcium, one ounce of cheese contains almost as much as ¾ of a cup of milk, about half the recommended daily ration for an adult.

Cheese provides high-quality proteins similar to those found in fish, meat, fowl, and eggs. An ounce of cheese has the same protein value as a large egg. As a main course, it is a very economical source of protein.

Here are some examples, and let us point out once again that hard cheeses have the greatest number of calories.

CHEESE	FAT CONTENT	PROTEIN	CALORIES *
Brie	about 25%	15%	325
Camembert	about 25%	20%	325
Emmenthal	about 30%	30%	400
Gruyère	about 30%	30%	400
Livarot	about 20%	30%	350
Parmesan	about 20%	40%	350
Port-Salut	about 30%	25%	350
Roquefort	about 25%	25%	325

* FOR A 3½ OUNCE PORTION (100G.)

3½ ounces of lean cheese contains on the average about 100 calories and about as much protein as 1 quart of milk.

2 ounces of cheese provides the recommended daily calcium ration for an adult.

It requires more than a gallon of milk to make one pound of cheese.

How to Buy Cheese

Many cheeses come in opaque packages and it is almost always impossible to choose among them. Therefore, one must place one s confidence in the manufacturers and resign oneself to buying in the same way as for a name brand bottle of wine, hoping that all the qualities that one expects are there. Still, a plastic, envelope does allow one to note the appearance of the cheese, and, if not buying in a supermarket, it is always possible to ask the merchant to open a box of Camembert in order to check its aroma and consistency. Here is some advice to follow on such occasions :

• A soft cheese should be felt all over, starting at the edge and working towards the center, which should be equally soft.

• A Brie or a Camembert should not be too soft or runny. Otherwise it will rapidly acquire a sharp taste.

• An odor of ammonia is the sign of a sharp or inedible Camembert.

• A Gruyère should not be too soft. This indicates poor aging and the cheese will probably have little or no flavor.

• A Gruyère in which the holes are moist should not be passed over. On the contrary, it is said to be " crying its salt " and is often better than another.

• A cheese which smells very strongly is not necessarily bad. It is only bad if it is not in its nature to have such a smell.

• All uncooked, pressed cheeses (Cantal, Saint-Paulin, etc.) should be uniform in color throughout. If this is not the case, it is because the fermentation was defective, and they risk being very sharp.

- Beware of semi-soft or hard cheeses which are deformed, swollen, or shrunken. They have continued to ferment and will be bitter or inedible.

All these precautions however, are only a first step, necessary without doubt, but still rather illusory. Two cheeses of the same make and apparently similar in all points can be as different as night and day. Just as the quality of a wine does not depend only on the professional skill of the vinegrower, that of milk (and thus of cheese) is subject to a great many conditions.

The breed of animal, its feed, the region, and the season of production are all determining factors. The moment of truth is the tasting of the cheese.

The label indicates the name of the manufacturer, the wholesaler or the retailer, the kind of cheese, its weight, and, if necessary, its age, flavor, and its type or nature (natural, cream, seasoning or mixture with other cheeses). Sometimes, the fat content and the degree of moisture are also mentioned. A successful buyer must pay attention to all these details. It is only thus that he will be able to make up his mind and choose with a degree of certainty the product that suits his needs.

If a refined or aged cheese costs slightly more than a mild cheese, it is because it must be stored — sometimes during a very long period — to acquire the desired quality (flavor, consistency) and this storage increases the cost price.

A sliced, rolled, or grated cheese requires more handling than the same cheese presented in a block and this additional preparation makes it necessarily more expensive.

Finally, the addition of foreign substances (fine herbs, fruit, aromatics) also increases the price of certain cheeses such as cottage cheese, yogurt, and cream cheese, which are less expensive in their natural state.

A final piece of advice : even though certain cheeses keep fairly well, never buy too far in advance. If the purchase is made in provision for a special dinner, or, even more important, for a cheese supper, it is best to buy several kinds, at least two more than the number of guests. It is possible to try to satisfy everybody's taste by choosing, as much as possible, cheeses which are different from one another in appearance, consistency, and flavor.

Keeping Cheese

The cheese cover has had its day. Old-fashioned and out of style, it is to be avoided for the successful keeping of cheese. Cheese should not be left in the dining-room or the kitchen. It is sensitive to the sun, to light, and to variations in temperature and humidity. To conserve a cheese, a piece of living matter which is continually worked on by yeasts and micro-organisms, is to try to keep it in prime condition by limiting as much as possible the decomposing action of the fermenting agents. The best temperature for this stabilization is between 41° and 50° F. The most practical place to keep it is in the crisper in the refrigerator.

A Word of Caution

- Before placing them in the refrigerator (crisper), wrap cheeses in one or more plastic bags.

- Cheeses should be neither touching nor placed one on top of the other.

- A goat's milk cheese, if preferred drier, should not be placed in plastic.

- If a soft-ripened cheese (Brie, Camembert, etc.) is too soft or runny, take it out of its box and dry it with a strong current of air (e.g., and electric hair dryer switched on to the cold air position). Then put it in the refrigerator.

- If a cheese of the same type does not seem to be ripe enough, take it out of its box, place it on a rack in a cool place and turn it over from time to time. Once the desired ripeness is obtained, put it in the refrigerator.

Hard cheeses (Cheddar, Swiss Cheese, etc.) are left in their original packages and well wrapped or placed in a covered container to prevent them from drying out. They will keep for several months in the refrigerator.

If a cheese has been cut into, wrap it carefully in plastic or aluminum foil. The presence of a mould on the surface of a hard cheese does not mean that it is inedible. Simply scrape it off before serving. If the cheese has become too dry and too hard, it can be grated for cooking and kept in an air-tight container.

Freezing protects cheeses against mould, and in the case of some of the more perishable ones, allows them to keep their flavor for a longer period of time. Since large pieces freeze with difficulty and risk crumbling when thawed, it is preferable to cut them into slices of no more than one pound in weight and one inch in thickness. These should then be tightly wrapped in a good quality plastic or aluminum foil and kept, frozen, at 0°F. It is not necessary to re-wrap cheeses which come in thick plastic or cardboard containers (such as Camembert).

Among the cheeses which can be frozen and kept at 0°F. for three months or more, let us mention the following: Brick Cheese, Blue Cheese, Caciocavallo, Camembert, Cheddar, Colby, Gouda, Limburger, Mozzarella, Oka, Parmesan, Provolone, Romano, Swiss Cheese, Tilsit, etc.

Freezing can, by accident, make some of them floury or crumbly, but they can still be used in salads or in preparing dishes where the texture of the cheese is of no importance.

One important thing : Cheeses should always be allowed to thaw in the refrigerator. Furthermore, to enjoy them at their best, they should be eaten at room temperature. Remove them from the refrigerator at least one hour before serving.

Cheese spreads will keep in the refrigerator for several weeks on condition that they are completely protected from the air (in a tightly-closed jar or a hermetic package).

When purchased in a box, a soft-ripened cheese with a washed crust (Pont-l'Evêque, Munster, Livarot, etc.) or a cheese with interior mould (Roquefort, Blue Cheese, Stilton, etc.) can be very effectively kept outside the refrigerator in its original wrapping and covered with a damp cloth (a maximum of three days).

We have already said that cheese keeps very well in the refrigerator. Do not forget, however, that some mild cheeses, which are more perishable, such as cottage cheese, yogurt, and cream cheese, should be eaten as fresh as possible. They will not keep for more than a few days and freezing is not very good for them either ; they quite rapidly become watery and floury.

General Rule

All cheeses should be eaten at room temperature. They should be removed from the refrigerator one hour before serving.

This lesson is undoubtedly well worth a cheese ?

— La Fontaine (Fable)

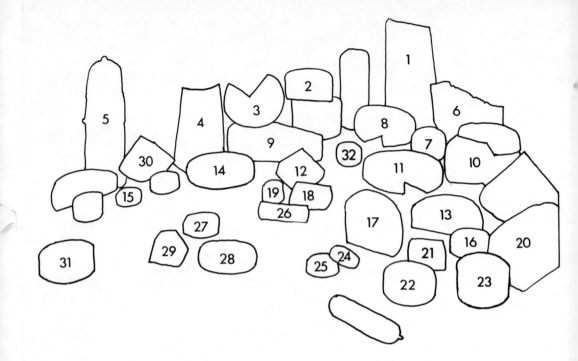

Some Famous French Cheeses

1- Emmenthal	12- Tome de Savoie (au Marc de Raisin)	22- Reblochon
2- Danish Blue	13- Reybier Noix	23- Stilton
3- St. Paulin	14- Brie	24- Banon
4- Canadian Cheddar	15- Baby Munster	25- Epoisses
5- Provolone	16- Jarlsberg	26- Ste. Maure
6- Gorgonzola	17- St. Benoit	27- Canadian Camembert
7- Edam	18- Pont l'Eveque	28- St. Nectaire
8- Pyranees	19- Boursault	29- Pyramide
9- Gruyere	20- Tilsit	30- Gouda
10- Cheshire	21- Camembert Disigny	31- Coulommiers
11- Oka		32- Baby Gouda

When to Serve It

Cheese can be offered on all occasions, at breakfast, at meals, and between meals. At meals, as a recipe ingredient, as a condiment, or natural, it can even figure throughout the course of a long and original menu, from the hors-d'œuvre to the dessert, passing via the appetizer and the main course. Between meals it is perfect as a good solid snack, to accompany an aperitif, or set off a cocktail or tea.

At Breakfast

Preference should be given to mild, nourishing, easily digestible cheeses (Cheddar, Jarlsberg, Edam, Gruyère, Norwegian Gjetost, Emmenthal, Comté).

With Meals

AS AN INGREDIENT :

Here are some that we suggest for certain cheese recipes :

- Fondue : Comté or Gruyère with a high fat content.
- Gratin : Comté or Parmesan.
- Béchamel Sauce : rather dry Comté (to avoid thickening of the sauce).
- Soufflé : Swiss Gruyère.
- Onion Soup : Comté.
- Spaghetti and other pastas : Parmesan and Gruyère in equal amounts so that the result is not too stringy (Parmesan does not go stringy). Add a bit of Comté to give the mixture a richer flavor.

● Welsh Rarebit : Cheshire or Cheddar.

Grated cheese (Parmesan, Swiss, natural or processed Cheddar) gives a pleasant lift to the flavor of many vegetables (asparagus, broccoli, cabbage, Brussel sprouts, cauliflower, carrots, celery, corn, eggplant, green beans, mushrooms, potatoes, squash, tomatoes). It can be sprinkled on vegetables which have been sautéed in butter or mixed with breadcrumbs and used to cover vegetables or a casserole before browning in the broiler.

A suggestion : Stuff vegetables (green peppers, onions, potatoes, squash, or tomatoes) with cooked rice or breadcrumbs mixed with grated cheese and spices.

AS A DESSERT :

As far as dessert cheeses are concerned, the choice is immense and our catalogue, even though incomplete, has something for every taste (see Part Two). After a spicy dish or after game, the best choice is still Camembert, Livarot, Pyramid, Blue, Roquefort, or Comté. A roast or a chicken requires instead a Brie, a Fourme d'Ambert, an Edam, or a Gruyère.

At what point in the meal should cheese be served ? Some people offer it at the same time as the salad. In England, it is presented at the end of dessert. However, the majority of connoisseurs agree in thinking that the most judicious place for it is just between the salad and the dessert proper.

As it neutralizes the acidity of vinegar or lemon, cheese paves the way for a better appreciation of the smoothness of a dessert which is always more or less sweet. Just the same, some cheese lovers prefer to renounce this kind of pleasure and finish off their meal with the flavor of cheese accompanied by a good wine.

As a Snack

Prepare either open- or close-faced sandwiches, lightly toasted or plain, and not too large. For an afternoon snack, use only mild cheeses. Some, such as Oka, when at room temperature spread almost as easily as butter. In the evening, a much vaster choice can be used, and one can even add various ingredients :

• Gruyère : round slices of pickle and hard-boiled egg placed between two thin slices of cheese.

• Cream cheese, cottage cheese, Mimolette : mix in finely chopped herbs (tarragon, parsley, chervil, chives). Salt and pepper lightly. Crushed walnuts can also be added.

• Emmenthal (grated) : mixed with creamy whipped butter.

• Leicester: with crushed walnuts.

• Roquefort: with raw or cooked egg-yolk.

As an Appetizer

Hors-d'œuvres served as appetizers should be light and small in size. They are only there to underline the bouquet and flavor of a given alcohol, and, on occasion, to neutralize the effect of drinking on an empty stomach.

Small cubes of Nökkel (a Norwegian cheese) go very well with port, Madeira, Banyuls, or a sweet vermouth. Cubes of Edam covered with celery salt or cocktail sausages stuffed with Gruyère are also appreciated. One can also fill the hollows of small pieces of celery stalk with a mixture of equal parts of Roquefort and butter. First remove the fibres from the celery, which should be both tender and crunchy.

With Cocktails

As a cocktail party usually occurs far enough away from a meal, one can use more substantial cheeses presented with imagination in the most diverse and amusing shapes: cubes, sticks, triangles, balls, etc. One can also prepare little ramekins (cheese melted in a mixture of red wine and spicy broth) or Roquefort toast spread with caviar and sprinkled with lemon juice.

To choose the wines which best accompany the suggested cheeses, see the Table of Wines further on in this book.

With Tea or Coffee

Mild cheeses are a must. Tea or coffee do not go well with flavors that are overly accentuated. Prepare mini-toasts with Caerphilly, Cheddar, Cheshire, Gjetost, etc.

How to Serve It

We have already condemned the use of a cheese cover. Presenting dessert cheeses on a plate is not really to be recommended if one wants to preserve a certain amount of decorum. Even if there is only one, it is preferable to serve it on a tray (wood, ceramic, plastic) or in a wicker basket with a wooden bottom. The cheese is never placed directly on the tray. One can put a lace or paper doily, a decoration of fresh leaves or, if necessary, a serviette under the cheese.

Cheese Trays

Making up a cheese tray involves anticipating the preferences of those for whom it is being made up, and whose tastes will by no means necessarily be the same. How many varieties should be used to make up a good tray ? This we have also mentioned before : two more than the number of guests is a reasonable number. At the same time, one should also be careful not to use too many cheeses of the same type (consistency and flavor), but this was already seen to at the time of buying.

Examples :

A FOUR CHEESE TRAY (2 soft and 2 dry cheeses)
Camembert — Roquefort — Comté — Gouda.

Or :
Coulommiers — Blue — Cantal — Cheddar.

A SIX CHEESE TRAY : (3 soft and 3 dry cheeses)
Brie — Stilton — Munster — Chevro-
tin — Edam — Emmenthal.

Or :
Vacherin — Pyramid — Gorgonzola — Tomme de Savoie —
Edam — Provolone.

Cheeses should be unwrapped before serving. Soft, downy crust cheeses should not be peeled in advance. Should hard-skinned cheeses be peeled ? A good question.

It is a matter of convenience not to peel them, and not an attempt to please those who relish their crust of Brie or Camembert, pretending that it is the best and richest part of the cheese, a veritable goldmine of vitamins and antibiotics. In truth, for the majority of cheeses, the crust is where the fermenting agents and moulds form and develop, and it should never be eaten.

Since cheeses must be eaten in the order of growing flavors, they can be placed on the tray according to this progression ; in a circle, for example, going from the mildest to the strongest. Some methodical hostesses take care to designate them with numbers or tags. This is undoubtedly a good precaution, but one which encounters varying amounts of enthusiasm. Some people find it very useful, while others feel that it is just a bit too much.

Even though the poet-prince, Charles of Orléans (1391-1465) had the strange custom of offering extremely strong cheeses to ladies towards whom he was in no way indifferent, an aggressive aroma often risks offending delicate noses. It would therefore be a good idea, if possible, to serve the more violent cheeses on a second tray. Finally, lean or diet cheeses should also be served apart, on a smaller tray.

Cheeses which have already been served and cut into at a preceding meal can be offered again. It is sufficient to tidy up their appearance by trimming them as necessary. If some of them show a tendency to run, it is prudent to stop this unattractive wandering with a small block of marble or a thin slat of wood.

After this is done, cover the trays with a damp cloth which will only be removed at the moment of serving. Do not forget to include a fork (indispensable for serving) and two knives, one for the mild cheeses and the other for the strong ones. If the tray has a Blue Cheese (Roquefort or other), also include a small, very thin knife, much more practical for cutting it.

Cheese is one of the most important elements of a well-balanced diet and nutritional experts recommend eating it at least three times a week.

(Canadian Department of Agriculture)

How to Appreciate It to the Fullest

At the same time as the cheese tray, one should also serve bread as well as various condiments for those who wish them : butter, mustard, etc. (since cheese is naturally salty, sweet butter is a preferable choice).

BREAD. A choice of white, rye, and black bread will answer to all tastes. However, good, coarse farmer's bread is usually the most appreciated. Pressed cheeses (Cantal, Cheshire, Gruyère, etc.) also work very well with crackers or very thin toast.

CONDIMENTS. Though condemned by all connoisseurs because they cover up the natural essence of a cheese, one must nevertheless be prepared to satisfy all the guests' wishes. This one might like to modify the sharpness of his Roquefort with butter ; another will want some mustard to add to the flavor of a Gruyère, an Emmenthal, or a Comté. What can one say about those who ask for pickles, ketchup, or HP sauce ? While advising that they should not be abused, here are some condiments that do go well with certain cheeses :

- Goat cheese, Demi-Sel, Saint-Marcellin : garlic, chives, shallots, walnuts.
- Cream cheese : parsley, tarragon, chervil, radishes.
- Cheshire, Comté, Holland : celery, olives, crushed walnuts.
- Munster : cumin, celery.
- Roquefort, Camembert : pearl onions.
- Process cream cheese : bananas, jam.

Though there are also trays in ceramics, glass, and plastic, it is still wood that provides the most attractive background on which to serve cheese. A small mat of straw or raffia can be added and, no matter what the color or the form of the cheese (wheel, point, slice, or whatever), it is certain that on this warm, rich bed it will be more appetizing.

The tray or trays will be made up of several kinds of cheese with different flavors and textures, all at room temperature, naturally. If there are a lot of guests, serve at least three varieties of mild cheese, and as many strong cheeses, allowing about a quarter of a pound per person. Remember that name tags, stuck in the cheeses often improve the appearance. One can also add, either served on the side or in among the cheeses, small bunches of grapes or slices of apples or pears.

Also make sure that there are plenty of crackers of different shapes and sizes, French bread both in roll and stick form, as well as sweet butter and even mustard to be sure not to have forgotten anything. Finally, a special platter, consisting solely of soft cheeses or cheese spreads and crackers is also certain to be very welcome.

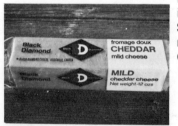

For the other trays, remember that Canadian mild cheeses include Brick Cheese, mild Cheddar, Colby, Gouda, Oka, Swiss Cheese, etc., and go best with light wines, either rosé or white. The strong cheeses are the blue cheeses, Camembert, old Cheddar, and Tilsit. They are served with port, sherry, and good, red tables wines.

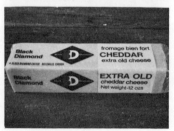

Tray Ideas

1) Place the cheeses in a circle , both the firm and the soft ones, both the mild and the strong — points of Camembert, circles of process cheese, cubes of strong Canadian Cheddar. A red-skinned Gouda will decorate the center of the tray. Garnish with fruit.

2) Place the points of Camembert in a star shape, surrounding them with points of Blue, slices of Swiss and Cheddar, and scatter small cubes of cream cheese throughout. Decorate with fruit.

With Which Wines ?

A very important factor in the serving of dinner is to make sure that one is not surprised by a prematurely dry wine cellar at the moment of serving the cheese. No matter how difficult, even at the risk of rather caustic comments, one must have the courage to hold back one or two bottles. Their appearance with the cheese tray will smooth over everything for the hitherto unfortunate and abused wine steward. But if a catastrophe does occur and everything runs out at once — wine, beer, and cider — then one is forced to console oneself with a simple glass of water. Water and cheese make the saddest of combinations, both on the tongue and in the stomach. An alcoholic beverage, black coffee, or even tea is preferable by far.

Furthermore, it is not necessary to offer as many different wines as there are kinds of cheese. Without speaking of the prohibitive cost of such an idea, it would greatly complicate the simple pleasure of savoring the cheese. For a tray where mild cheeses are in the majority, a single good wine, well-chosen, is very able to do the job. The only exception, if one wants to be finicky, might be a very strong Blue Cheese, which could use an old, full-bodied Burgundy.

Some Wines That Go Well With Cheese

Burgundy	(Barbera, Gamay, Pinot red or black, etc.) Wines which are all designed to accompany an old Cheddar served as a dessert or in the main dish.

Chablis	Less acid than a Rhine wine and delicious with a cheese soufflé.
Champagne	Serve, either white or pink, with a good cheesecake.
Chianti	A famous dry Italian wine that is a choice companion for spaghetti with cheese.
Claret	Milder and lighter than the Burgundies, the clarets **(Cabernet, Zinfandel, etc.)** are excellent with a soufflé, a fondue, and with all dishes made with mild cheese.
Muscatel	A lovely red or golden wine, with a pronounced bouquet. Should be served with a process cheese spread and crackers.
Port	Rich, thick, and very sweet (white port is a bit less so), it goes very well with a tray of cheese and fruit.
Rosé	A wine that is light and fruity, it goes well with any cheese.
Sauterne	Dry or semi-sweet, it can be served with all cheese dishes, especially if they are not too strong.
Sherry	Dry or semi-sweet, it is delicious with all cheese-based cocktail canapés.
Tokay	A lovely, rose-amber liqueur wine, much less sweet than a port. Rather, it should be served, like muscatel, with a process cheese spread.
Vermouth	A highly perfumed wine that is best served " on the rocks ". Should be used to accompany a cheese spread or a cheese dip.
Rhine Wine	**(Riesling, Traminer, Folle Blanche, Sylvaner, etc.)** With a snack or with dessert, with Camembert, Swiss Cheese, or mild Cheddar.

Man has not yet found anything that accompanies a cheese better than wine.

— Pierre Androuet

Table of Wines

N.B. These are only suggestions and all experiments are permissible. It is only thus that discoveries are made.

CHEESES :	WINES :
Fresh Cheeses (Demi-Sel, Petit-Suisse, Suprême, etc.)	Not necessary (a dry white or rosé may be used)
Soft Downy Crust Cheeses (Brie, Camembert, Coulommiers, etc.)	Fruity red wines with a good bouquet (Vougeot, Médoc, Chinon, Nuits, Volnay, etc.)
Soft Cheeses with a Washed Crust (Livarot, Munster, Maroilles, etc.)	Robust wines with a generous bouquet (Hermitage, Corton, Saint-Emilion, etc.)
Mouldy Cheeses (Blue Cheeses, Roquefort, etc.)	Strong, full-bodied wines (Pouzy, Pomerol, Chambertin, Chateauneuf-du-Pape, Haut-Brion, etc.)
Goat's-milk Cheeses (Sainte-Maure, Chavignol, etc.)	Very dry white wines or light reds (Pouilly, Chablis, Sancerre, Muscadet, Moulin-à-Vent, Pinot, etc.)
Semi-Soft Cheeses (Saint-Paulin, Tomme, Oka, etc.)	Light, tender whites or rosés (Beaujolais, Arbois, Anjou, Touraine, etc.)
Hard Cheeses (Emmenthal, Comté, Gruyère, etc.)	Dry whites or perfumed reds (Muscadet, Mâcon, etc.)

An enjoyable " beer and cheese " tasting in the reception
rooms of Labatt Breweries.

Wine is Not the Only Answer

Even though wine is the perfectly designed companion for cheeses, beer, cider, liquor, etc. can also be instrumental in its appreciation.

Following the example of '' wine and cheese '' parties, it has become common in Canada to organize get-togethers of the same kind where beer takes the place of the noble juice of the vine.

The number of cheeses that can be properly savored with beer is vast enough to satisfy the most exacting gastronomes.

Here are some beers that can be offered with cheese :

Heavy Ales :

Strong or blue cheeses. Cheshire, Imperial, Ermite, Saint-Benoit (Blue), Roquefort, strong Cheddar, Danish Blue, etc.

Light Ales :

Italian cheeses, as well as dry, white cheeses. Gouda, mild Cheddar, Edam, Port-Salut and its relatives, Saint-Paulin, Emmenthal, Gruyère, etc.

Lager Beers :

Pomme de Savoie, Brie, Oka, Carré de l'Est, Délices des Moines and others of its type, Boursault, Tartares, process cream cheese with herbs, flavored with Kirsch, etc.

Here are a Few Experiments to Try :

Beer	with	Appenzell, Camembert, Cheshire, Cheddar, Comté, Edam, Emmenthal, Gouda, Gruyère, Gloucester, Lancashire, Leyde, Livarot, Maroilles, Norbo, Petit-Suisse, Tilsit.
Cider	with	Camembert, Livarot, Pont-l'Evêque.
Champagne	with	Délice, Suprême.
Port	with	Cheddar, Cheshire, Mimolette, Nökkel, Parmesan.
Asti Spumante	with	Parmesan.
Spirits	with	Livarot, Roquefort.
Black Coffee	with	Maroilles.
Tea	with	Caerphilly, Cheddar, Cheshire, Chester.
Chocolate	with	Gjetost.

Part two

A CATALOGUE OF CHEESES

If I had a son who was thinking of marriage, I would say to him : Beware of the young girl who likes neither wine, nor truffles, nor cheese, nor music.

COLETTE

Before Consulting
the Catalogue

We have taken a look at the history of cheese, the diverse methods of making it, its nutritional potential, how to buy it, keep it, serve it, and enjoy it. We are now better informed, but let us hesitate before displaying our rather elementary knowledge. We run the risk of forgetting that by far the most important thing is the tasting pleasure that it can and should provide us with.

The following catalogue contains, in dictionary form, the principal cheeses that are relatively easy to obtain. Once again, it is far from being a complete list, but the 122 varieties that it proposes provide an ample choice. Chance and curiosity will lead to the discovery of others that are every bit as succulent. Their many forms and origins will render the discovery even more interesting. Among other information, we indicate briefly the peculiarities, the qualities, and the eventual weaknesses of each cheese. The indications regarding the wines that should accompany them are only suggestions and are not absolute rules. And finally, here and there are to be found recipes in which cheese plays an important part.

Anfrom

Uses : Desserts, snacks, croque-monsieur, appetizers.

Characteristics : Extra-fat (48-50%). Pronounced flavor. Light brown crust with white overtones. Cheese is yellow, pressed, semi-soft.

Related cheese : Oka.

Appearance : Comes in a 6 lb. wheel, a baby wheel of 14 ounces and a mini-wheel of 8 ounces. Also available in plastic-wrapped points of 8 oz.

How to enjoy it : With red wine or beer.

Historical background : Manufactured in Quebec since 1957 and perfected by Mr. Loevenbruck.

Appenzel (or Bloderkäse)

Uses : Quite varied. Desserts, snacks, cooking.

Origin : Switzerland (Appenzel Canton).

Characteristics : Made from the milk of mountain cattle. Fat (45%). Flavor that runs from mild to pronounced, creamier than Tilsit. Brushed crust. A hard cheese that is pressed and cooked. Riddled with small round holes. There is also an Appenzel that is less rich, called ¼ fat, with a harsher taste.

Appearance : Comes in convex-sided wheels of 10 to 15 lbs. Sold by weight and in pre-wrapped portions.

How to choose it : Gives off little odor. The crust should be even and smooth ; the interior very firm. Beware of a crust that is cracked or a cheese that is too hard and crumbly unless you are only looking for a strong cheese to use for cooking.

How to enjoy it : With a fruity red wine or beer.

" Appenzel Chäshappe "

Makes enough to serve four people :

5¼ oz. of thinly sliced Appenzel
4 eggs
1 cup of milk
1 small cup of beer
½ tsp. of yeast
4 tbsp. of flour

Melt the cheese in the milk over a low heat while stirring continuously.

Allow to cool.

Make a dough from the flour, the yeast, and the beer, adding the eggs one at a time.

Mix these two preparations.

Place some frying oil in a large frying pan and heat to the boiling point. Pour the mixture into the boiling oil through a funnel, so as to obtain long sausages. Once these (chäshappes) have turned a light brown, drain and serve very hot with a salad.

REMARKS :

Asiago

Uses : A handy all-round semi-fat cheese. Good as a dessert or grated for seasoning.

Origin : Italy (Vicenza). Takes its name from the Asiago Plateau where it is made.

Characteristics : Made from cow's milk. Semi-fat (30%) ; also comes extra-fat under the name of '' Asiago da allievo ''. Rather pleasant, sharp flavor. Brushed crust. The cheese is hard, pressed, uncooked, and has holes.

Related cheese : Montasio.

Appearance : Comes in slightly convex-sided wheels of 17 to 27 lbs. Sold by weight and in pre-wrapped portions.

Beware of a cheese that is too swarthy or too crumbly unless it is to be used only as a condiment.

How to choose it : Gives off little odor. The crust is smooth, even, and supple ; the cheese straw-colored, granular, and elastic, with well-spaced, medium-sized holes.

How to enjoy it : With a Chantigue, or with a fruity or full-bodied Italian wine, depending on the ripeness of the cheese.

REMARKS :

Banon

Uses : Widespread, mostly as a dessert cheese.

Origin : France (Provence, Dauphiné). From the village of Banon in the lower Alps.

Characteristics : Made from the milk of goats, sheep, or cows. Fat (45%) or extra-fat (55%). Mild nutty flavor. Natural crust. The cheese is soft and uncooked.

Related cheeses : All sheep, cow, or goat cheeses that are aged in leaves.

Appearance : Wrapped in chestnut leaves and tied with raffia. Comes in a small disc of 3 oz. Available in natural, pepper, savory, curry, or paprika flavors.

How to choose it : Gives off a rather strong odor. The crust should be a bit sticky, the cheese firm and supple. Be careful of a crust that smells strongly of fermentation, and of a cheese that is granular or too salty.

How to enjoy it : With a fruity wine ; either red, white or rosé.

Baron de Caravettes

An extra-fat cheese spread (48%).

Very delicate flavor, slightly augmented by a mixture of seven aromatic herbs (garlic, onion, parsley, etc.).

Comes in a small, 6 oz. plastic pot.

Good with a dry or semi-sweet wine (red or rosé), or cider.

REMARKS :

Beaumont

Uses : Widespread, desserts, cheese snacks.

Origin : France (Savoy).

Characteristics : Made from cow's milk. Extra-fat (50%). Mild, creamy taste. Washed crust. Cheese is semi-firm, pressed, uncooked.

Related cheeses : Saint-Paulin, Oka, Anfrom.

Appearance : Comes in a flat, wrapped, 3 lb. disc. Available cut to order and in prepared pre-wrapped portions.

How to choose it : Gives off no particular odor. The light yellow crust must be even, supple, and delicate ; the cheese must be uniform in color.

Beware of a swollen, fermented, or dried out crust ; this means that the cheese has been poorly kept or is too old, and it will be bitter.

How to enjoy it : With Beaujolais, a fruity white wine.

REMARKS :

Bel Paese

Uses : Widespread. Very digestible and nourishing. Good for desserts, sandwiches, croque-madame.

Origin : Italy (Lombardy). Its name is a trademark.

Characteristics : Made from cow's milk. Extra-fat (48%). Mild, delicate flavor. Washed crust. Cheese is tender, pressed, uncooked.

Related cheeses : Saint-Paulin, Oka, Port-Salut, Anfrom.

Appearance : Comes in foil-wrapped, labelled wheels of 4 to 5 lbs. Also in small wheels of a little more than a pound under the name of Bel Paesino. Also sold to order and in prepared portions.

How to choose it : Gives off a pleasant, milky odor. The creamy yellow cheese is soft.

Be careful of a fermented crust. The cheese risks being sharp.

How to enjoy it : With a Valpolicella.

Historical background : Originally manufactured by the

Chartreuse monks of Pavia. Its international distribution is quite recent.

Berka

Uses : Desserts, snacks.

Origin : Western Canada.

Characteristics : Extra-fat (48-50%). Hard crust. Semi-firm, whitish, lightly salted cheese. This is a new cheese of the " Trappist " type, resembling Oka and Saint-Paulin, but sharper and less creamy. Will keep for 2-3 months.

Appearance : In wheels of 3 lbs. or 6 oz.

How to choose it : The crust must be hard.

How to enjoy it : With a dry wine, either a red Bordeaux or a white Rhine wine or Moselle.

Bonne Mère

A soft extra-fat cheese (48%).
Made from cow's milk, using a very old recipe from Provence (France) which originally called for sheep or goat's milk.

Spiced and peppered.

Comes in 5 oz. portions packed in a small orange and brown cardboard box.

Goes well with á dry or semi-sweet wine (red or rosé), or with cider.

REMARKS :

Bresse Bleu or Bleu De Bresse

Uses : A very good dessert cheese (by itself or with fresh fruit).

Origin : France (Bresse). There are also excellent blue cheeses from Canada, Denmark, Norway, England, Italy, and Germany (Edelpilz).

Characteristics : Made from cows' milk. Extra-fat (48-50%). Made in a similar fashion to Roquefort. Strong, sharp, peppery flavor. Natural crust. The cheese is soft, uncooked, with blue-green marbling produced by a mould the '' penicillium '' of rye bread. Recommended for those who do not like wishy-washy cheeses.

Related cheeses : Other Blues (d'Auvergne, des Causses), Gorgonzola, Stilton.

Appearance : Comes in a flat round disc, wrapped in foil inside a wooden sheath. There are three formats : 16 oz., 8 oz., and the 4 oz. '' Bressinet ''.

Danish Blue : In 5 and 6 pound wheels. Sold in points by desired weight.

Norwegian Blue : In 5-6 pound wheels. Sold in prepared 4 oz. points.

How to choose it : Gives off a slight smell of mould. The thin crust is blue and white ; the cheese is white, supple, and oily, with well-separated veins running through it.

Beware of a sticky crust or a greyish or reddish cheese ; it will be too strong. N.B. Canadian blue is semi-firm and a bit crumbly.

How to enjoy it : With a Hermitage, a Tavel, or a Chateauneuf-du-Pape.

Cheese Delights

To make about 30 delights :

⅓ cup of crumbled blue cheese

8 oz. of cream cheese

1 tbsp. of finely chopped onion

A few drops of hot sauce, mayonnaise

¼ cup of crushed corn flakes

Pretzel sticks

Mix the cheeses, the onion, and the hot sauce.

Add enough mayonnaise to make the mixture easy to shape.

Roll into balls and coat with crushed corn flakes.

Place in refrigerator.

Just before serving, spear the balls with pretzel sticks.

REMARKS :

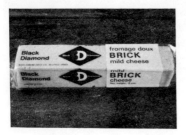

Brick

Uses : Desserts, sandwiches.

Characteristics : Extra-fat (48-50%). Has a bitter tasting, caramel colored crust. The creamy yellow cheese is semi-hard, plastic, and pierced with numerous small holes. Its flavor is reminiscent of a ripened cheese of the Tilsit or Port-Salut type and it becomes very strong with aging.

Related cheese : Munster.

How to enjoy it : Brick fanciers prefer beer to the usual companion of cheese, which is wine, but any red or rosé wine goes well enough with it.

Historical background : Created by accident in 1877 by an American cheese-maker of Swiss descent, John Jossi, of Dodge County, Wisconsin. While making Limburger, the specialty of his business, he noticed that if the curds were heated to a lower temperature, the result was a cheese with a different texture. Brick was born.

REMARKS :

Brie

Uses : Diverse. Desserts, (by itself or accompanied by fresh fruit), canapés, croquettes, vol-au-vents.

Origin : France (Brie). Canadian and German Bries also exist.

Characteristics : Made from cow's milk. Fat (45%). Mild, delicate, nutty flavor. Downy crust. The cheese is soft and lightly salted, neither cooked nor pressed.

Related cheese : Camembert, Coulommiers.

Appearance : Comes in a 4 or 5 lb. wheel. It is sold by weight ; in a triangular box (a point of 3 or 4 oz.); squares (5 or 8 oz.) ; an oval (7 oz.) ; a Brie Rectangle (6 oz.) ; and a Baby Rectangle (3 oz.).

Canadian Brie : Comes in 5 lb. wheels, retailed in 4 oz. points.
German Brie : Comes in a two portion box (4½ oz.).

How to choose it : Gives off a faint smell of fungus. The crust should be covered with white down, slightly pigmented with reddish-brown ; the supple oily cheese should be straw-colored.

Beware of a crust that is too white or too red ; of an interior paste that is hard, granular, or flaky. The cheese will be too salty and bitter.

Note : In the case of an entire wheel of 4 or 5 lbs. the thinner half, better ripened, is the best choice. Since Brie is put out to dry on an inclined plane, there is a slight sliding of the paste towards the bottom, and this part, becoming thicker, ages more slowly.

How to enjoy it : With any of the red wines of Bordeaux, Burgundy, or Côtes-du-Rhône.

Historical background : Already a favorite of Charlemagne in 774 A.D., Queen Marie Leczinska, wife of Louis XV, used Brie de Coulommiers to prepare her famous vol-au-vents. At the Congress of Vienna, in 1815, while a com-

bined Europe decided the fate of France and Napoleon after the battle of Waterloo, the Austrian chancellor, Metternich, had the good taste (or the sense of irony) to proclaim Brie the king of the world's cheeses.

REMARKS:

Brie (Canadian)

Uses: Desserts, (by itself or with fresh fruit), canapés, croquettes, vol-au-vents.

Type: French.

Characteristics: Extra-fat (48%). Light brown crust; the creamy colored interior is smooth and elastic, from mild to strong in flavor, according to the degree of ripeness.

Related cheeses: Camembert, Carré de l'Estrie.

Appearance: Comes in a 5 lb. wheel and in a 4 ounce point.

How to enjoy it: With a light red or a sparkling wine.

REMARKS:

Caciocavallo

Uses : Good for desserts and snacks when it is young. Old and grated : a cooking condiment.

Origin : Italy. Undoubtedly draws its name from the fact that at one time it was made from mare's milk. A Canadian-made Caciocavallo can be found.

Characteristics : Made from cow's milk. Fat (44%). It has a flavor that is mild, delicate, and slightly smoky. Natural crust that is dried and oiled. The uncooked paste is pressed, poured, and often smoked.

Related cheese : Provolone.

Appearance : Comes in a gourd shape that is about 5 inches in diameter by 14 to 16 inches in height. Weight : 6½ to 9 lbs. It is retailed according to the amount desired.

How to choose it : Gives off a slight smoky odor. The crust is thin, smooth, even, going from light yellow to golden in color. The ivory white paste is compact and a bit supple. Be careful of a cheese that has holes and is sharp, though some people do prefer it this way.

How to enjoy it : With a Chianti or a Valpolicella.

Historical background : It must have been imported into Europe by the barbarian invasions of the 6th century.

REMARKS :

Caciocavallo (Canadian)

Uses : Desserts and snacks when it is soft. When hard, it is usually used grated for cooking.

Type : Italian.

Characteristics : Fat. A white paste that is firm and smooth, with a light brown, hard crust. The flavor is mild, becoming nutty with age.

Related cheeses : Scamorza, Provolone.

Appearance : Comes in a 4 lb. ball with a neck allowing the cheese to be hung up to dry.

How to enjoy it : With red wine (Chianti, Valpolicella).

REMARKS :

Caerphilly

Origin : England.

Characteristics : Made from cow's milk. The paste is creamy white, semi-soft, pierced by the odd hole. Mild taste.

Appearance : Comes in a plastic-wrapped 8 pound wheel and a 1 pound mini-cheese.

How to enjoy it : With tea and sticks of raw celery.

REMARKS :

Camembert

Uses : Multiple. Desserts, snacks, canapés, croquettes.

Origin : France (Normandy). From the village of Camembert. There are also Camemberts made in Canada, Denmark, Switzerland, Germany, etc.

Characteristics : Made from cow's milk. Extra-fat (45-50%). Slight milky taste. White downy crust with superficial mould, sometimes pigmented with red or brown. Soft paste, slightly salty, that is subject to neither cooking, pressing, nor kneading. When at its peak, Camembert (as well as Brie) has a reputation for restoring the intestinal balance partially destroyed by the use of medicinal antibiotics.

Related cheeses : Brie, Coulommiers, Carré de l'Est.

Appearance : Comes in round boxes of 4 and 8 ounces, in

63

a box containing 6 points (8 oz.), and in a half moon (demi-camembert) of 4 ounces.

Canadian Camembert : In round boxes of 4 and 8 ounces, and in boxes of 3 and 8 portions.

German Camembert : In a 2 portion box (4½ oz.).

Danish Camembert : In boxes of 4 and 7 ounces. Camembert Swiss fondue : In a 4 ounce box.

How to choose it : Gives off a good fungus odor. It should be well-formed, flat, cylindrical ; the paste firm and slightly flexible throughout. Camembert, even when ripe, should never run. Running comes from improper drying in the manufacturing process. Furthermore, it will empty and is then no longer edible.

Beware of any odor of ammonia, or of a crust that is hollow or overly brown around the edges. The cheese has altered and will be very sharp.

How to enjoy it : With a good red table wine ; a Vougeot, an Haut-Brion, or even beer.

Historical background : Discovered around 1790 by Marie Harel, a farmer's wife from the village of Camembert. Wrapped only in straw, it was much too vulnerable to travel any distance at all. It was only in 1890 that an ingenious inventor, Mr. Ridel, thought of giving it its famous little round box which was responsible for its becoming universally known. From that point on, well-secured in its package, it was able to leave on its conquest of the world. In 1928, thanks to the generosity of the cheese-makers of Ohio, a statue was erected in Vimoutiers (Normandy) in memory of Marie Harel. There is no statue for Mr. Ridel.

A country which has 325 varieties of cheese to offer is a country that is impossible to govern.

— Winston Churchill

Norman Devils

1 fat Camembert
1½ oz. of butter
1 tbsp. of flour, well rounded
1 tbsp. of rice, well rounded
1 teacup of milk
Egg white
Breadcrumbs
Salt and pepper
Frying oil

Melt the butter, add to it the flour and the rice, then the milk, the salt and the pepper.

Bring to a boil, stirring constantly, until a thick paste is obtained.

Cut the Camembert into cubes from which the crust has been removed and add it to the paste.

Spread the mixture on a well-greased and floured cookie sheet to a depth of ¾ of an inch.

Allow to cool. Cut into discs, dip in egg white, and twice in breadcrumbs.

When ready to serve, fry in boiling oil.

REMARKS :

Camembert (Canadian)

Uses : Desserts, snacks, canapés, croquettes.

Type : French.

Characteristics : Extra-fat (48%). Manufactured according to the process conceived in the 18th century by a Norman farmer's wife, Marie Harel (née Fontaine). Has a greyish-white mouldy crust. The paste is creamy when ripe. The flavor is mild to sharp, depending on the age.

Appearance : Comes in a round box of 8 ounces (Madame Clement, Gros Normand) ; of 4 oz. (Petit Normand). Also available in an 8 portion box (Gros Normand) or a 3 portion box (Madame Clement).

How to enjoy it : With a red or a white wine, a sweet wine, a sparkling wine, or beer.

REMARKS :

Cancoillotte

Uses : Very practical. Spread on toast.

Origin : France (Franche-Comté).

Characteristics : Made from skimmed cow's milk. Lean (20%). Obtained from a mixture of fresh butter, salty water, and Metton (a cheese with a fat content of 1%).

Appearance : Comes in a 15 ounce box.

How to enjoy it : Warm. One can flavor it with garlic or white wine. The skin which forms on the surface when it is warmed up should be as smooth as possible ; the paste should be light yellow or have a slight greenish tinge.

Beware of a grey Cancoillotte : it has turned.

Wine is not necessary, but a fruity white Anjou will do very nicely.

66

Cantal or Fourme de Cantal

Uses : Extremely practical. Good for desserts, snacks, and as a condiment for soups, gratins, sauces, purées (truffades).

Origin : France (Auvergne). Gets its name from the Cantal Mountains, where it comes from.

Characteristics : Made from the milk of high-mountain cattle. Fat (45%). Nutty, mild flavor. Natural brushed crust. Paste is pressed, but not cooked. With a pronounced perfume, it is a favorite of connoisseurs. Very digestible, it is also good for those with delicate stomachs, for the sick, and for children.

How to choose it : The crust, which gives off a faint odor of caves, is light grey, without cracks, or a darker grey and slightly wrinkled. The paste is compact, more or less supple, depending on the age, and has a very pronounced milky smell.

Beware of a cracked pitted crust ; of a paste which is not even throughout ; the cheese will be very sharp.

How to enjoy it : With a Beaujolais, Tavel, Hermitage, Chateauneuf-du-Pape.

Historical background : One of the oldest of cheeses, it was well-known in ancient Rome.

Truffade

To serve 6 to 8 persons :

11 oz. of Cantal
3 lb. 5 oz. of potatoes cut into discs
3 tbsp. of oil
Lard
Salt

Melt a bit of lard in a frying pan and add the oil.

Add the sliced potatoes and cook over low heat for about one half hour, without allowing them to brown.

Mash the potatoes well and add the Cantal, which has been cut into small pieces.

Stir the mixture for 10 minutes until the cheese is well mixed throughout.

Remove the excess fat, allow to brown on the bottom, and turn out onto a plate to serve.

Gatiss (Cheese Turnovers)

With pastry dough, shape a small pancake and cover it to a depth of ¾ of an inch with a mixture of one part Blue Cheese, one part Gruyère, and one part Cantal.

Sprinkle with paprika. Fold over the dough, and bake in the oven as for a pie until golden brown.

REMARKS :

Capucin

Uses : Snacks, desserts.

Characteristics : Extra-fat (50%). Very mild flavor. The crust is ochre, the pressed paste is a yellowish color. Recommended for children.

Appearance : Comes in a plastic-wrapped, 8 ounce wheel.

How to enjoy it : With white wine, cider, or beer.

Historical background : Made in Quebec since 1964 and perfected by M. Loevenbruck, who is carrying on the work of his father and his grandfather, descendants of a long line of French master cheese-makers.

REMARKS :

Cardinal

Uses : Desserts, snacks, appetizers.

Characteristics : Extra-fat (48-50%). A natural cheese that then undergoes special preparation and aging processes. Washed crust ; soft lightly-colored cheese that is pierced with small holes. Typical mild flavor.

Appearance : Comes in a 3 or 4 lb. loaf, a 1 pound wheel, and in an 8 oz. stick.

Historical background : Developed in the province of Quebec in the early 1930's. It was perfected by Dr. Rosell, a

bacteriologist and specialist in problems dealing with milk, with the collaboration of the St-Hyacinthe Institute of Agricultural Technology, and baptized '' Le Cardinal '' by Mr. J.F. Desmarais.

REMARKS :

Carré de l'Est

Uses : Very handy. Good for dessert, snacks.

Origin : France (Champagne, Lorraine). Takes its name from its shape and from the geographical location of the provinces where it is manufactured. There is also a Canadian-made Carré de l'Est. (Carré de l'Estrie).

Characteristics : Made from cow's milk. From fat to extra-fat (40-50%). Mild flavor similar to that of Brie or Camembert. Has a downy mould crust. The paste is soft, slightly salty, and neither cooked, pressed, nor kneaded.

Related cheeses : Camembert, Brie, Coulommiers.

Appearance : Comes in boxes of 8 ounces and 5 ounces.

How to choose it : Gives off a faint odor of mushrooms. The crust should be very white and downy, the cheese soft but not runny.

Be careful of a crust that is grey or is too streaked with red, as well as of a paste that is either dried out or runny.

How to enjoy it : With any good, light, red wine (Burgundy).

REMARKS :

Carré de l'Estrie

Uses : Desserts, snacks.

Type : French. Known in France under the name '' Carré de l'Est ''. In Canada, it is manufactured in the Eastern Townships of Quebec. Hence the name '' l'Estrie '' (The Eastern Townships).

Characteristics : Extra-fat (48%). Downy mould crust and a soft paste with a flavor reminiscent of Brie or Camembert.

Appearance : Comes in square boxes of 8 or 5 ounces.

How to enjoy it : With a light red wine.

REMARKS :

Chambarand or Chambarand Trappist

Uses : Quite handy. Desserts.

Origin : France (Dauphiné). Takes its name from the Trappist monastery of Chambarand at Roybon.

Characteristics : Made from cow's milk. Fat (45%). Mild, creamy flavor. Washed crust. The paste is soft, slightly pressed, and uncooked.

Related cheeses : Reblochon, Saint-Paulin, Oka, etc.

Appearance : Comes in a round 6 ounce box.

How to choose it : Gives off no particular odor. The crust is smooth, light yellow or light pink ; the paste is tender, soft, and of the same color throughout.

Beware of a cheese that is swollen, that smells of fermentation, that has a paste that is granular or dry. It will be bitter.

How to enjoy it : With a Chasseles, a Sancerre, a Mâcon.

REMARKS :

Champignon (Camembert or Brie)

Uses : Desserts, snacks.

Origin : West Germany (Bavaria).

Characteristics : A designation that groups two types of cheese, Camembert, and Brie. Both are extra-fat (50%).

Appearance : Champignon Camembert — in a round cardboard box with 2 portions (4½ oz.) ; with 6 portions (11 oz.). Also comes in a 2 portion metal box allowing preservation for up to 12 months (4½ oz.).

Champignon Rham-Brie — in a triangular cardboard box containing 1 portion (3½ oz.) ; in a 2 portion round metallic box under the name of Briette (4½ oz.).

REMARKS :

Cheddar

Uses : Very handy for desserts, snacks, canapés, soups, salads, and seasoning.

Origin : England (Somerset). Takes its name from the Cheddar Valley where it came from originally. There are also cheddars of Canadian, Australian, American, and New Zealand manufacture, but these should more accurately be called Cheshire (see listing).

Characteristics : Made from cow's milk. Extra-fat. Mild nutty flavor that becomes more accentuated and sharper with age. Natural greased crust. The paste is pressed and is neither cooked nor colored.

Related cheeses : Colby, Dunlop, Killarney, Monterey, Chester, Leicester, Gloucester.

Appearance : Comes in a cheesecloth-wrapped cylinder of about 140 to 165 pounds. It is retailed in blocks or points of varying weights. Canadian Cheddar : old (block or point of 5 pounds) ; mild (block or point of 5, 10, or 18 lbs.) ; process (block of 5 pounds). All are also retailed by desired weight.

How to choose it : Gives off a faint, pleasant odor. The crust should be even and not too waxy. With age, the colour of the cheese changes from a creamy white to a dark orange. At first smooth, firm, oily, and a bit soft, it hardens and becomes crumbly.

Unless a very sharp cheese is desired, be careful of a cheese that is overly hard, very granular, and very crumbly.

How to enjoy it : With a Bordeaux, port, beer, or tea.

Cheese Soup

To serve four :

2 cups of grated strong cheddar
3 tbsp. of melted butter
2 cups of milk
1 cup of chopped onions
1 cup of diced celery
1 tbsp. of flour
3 strips of fried bacon, well crumbled
1 tsp. of dry mustard
Paprika, salt, and pepper

Sauté the onions and celery in butter for about 5 minutes.

Add the flour, the spices, and then, bit by bit, the milk.

Cook while stirring well until the soup thickens.

Add the cheese and continue stirring until it melts.

Garnish with bacon and serve immediately.

Cheddar (Canadian)

Uses : Desserts, snacks, canapés, sandwiches, cooking (sauces, salads, main dishes).

Type : English.

Characteristics : Made from whole milk. Semi-fat (32-34%). It is the only cheese that is divided into types (according to its flavor, texture, and color). It must conform to standards concerning both fat content and humidity.

Three weeks after its manufacture, federal inspectors divide it into 3 categories. Only top-quality Cheddar can be sold under this name. The others which are still cheeses of value, will be processed, emulsified or heated and reworked in diverse manners. They will be used to make derivatives such as process cheese, Cream O Lack (see listing), État Kosher (hickory smoked, 27.5% fat content, sold in 8 ounce packages), etc.

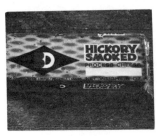

The Cheddar itself is offered for sale under three different labels : mild, medium, and strong (or old). The "mild" is a young Cheddar that is 2 to 3 months old ; 4 to 5 months of aging gives the "medium" — a more full-bodied flavor ; the "strong" has been allowed to reach its full maturity, which can take anywhere from 9 months to 2 years. The color of Cheddar, depending on its age, varies between cream and dark orange. In general, the paste of a strong Cheddar has no coloring added. An absolute rule : A Good Cheddar should never be bitter.

Appearance : Comes in loaves or points of 5, 10, and 18 pounds. Also in plastic-wrapped 8 oz. portions. Process Cheddar (orange in color and mild to sharp in flavor) is available in 5 lb. loaves and in prepared portions. There is also a grain Cheddar (see listing on Grain Cheese).

How to enjoy it : With red or rosé wine, smooth if the Cheddar is mild (claret, rosé, etc.), more full-bodied if it is strong (Chianti, Burgundy, Gamay, etc.).

Historical background : First made in the English village whose name it bears, Cheddar was introduced to Canada by the United Empire Loyalists. At first made at the farm level, its production became industrialized only in 1864, when the first cheese factory was built in Ingersoll, Ontario. In spite of the innumerable types of cheeses, Canadian or otherwise, offered today to Canadian

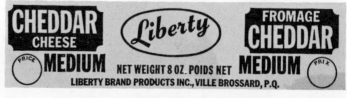

cheese lovers, Cheddar still is the most popular. By itself, it represents about two-thirds of the total consumption of the country.

Cheddar Soufflé

For 6 people :

1 ⅓ cups of grated Cheddar
1 cup of milk
¼ cup of all-purpose flour
4 beaten egg yolks
4 egg whites
3 tbsp. of butter
Salt and pepper

Melt the butter, and mix in the flour, salt, and pepper.

Add the milk, little by little, while stirring, until the mixture thickens (about 5 minutes).

Add the Cheddar.

Remove from heat and gradually add the egg yolks.

Allow to cool until lukewarm.

Beat the whites until they are firm without being dry.

Mix the sauce with the whites and pour into an ungreased casserole dish.

Brown at 325°F. (55-60 minutes) or poach at 350°F. (1 hour).

Serve quickly.

Cheddar Sauce

For vegetables, hard-boiled eggs, macaroni, fish.

Required ingredients :
1 cup of grated Cheddar

¼ cup of flour
2 cups of milk
½ tsp. of dry mustard
¼ cup of butter
Salt, pepper, and paprika

Melt the butter, and add the flour and the spices.

Add the milk gradually while stirring without stopping to obtain a sauce that is thick and smooth.

Add the cheese and keep stirring so that it melts evenly.

Just before serving, beat vigorously.

The sauce can then be poured over vegetables, hard-boiled eggs, macaroni, or fish, and put in the broiler to brown.

REMARKS:

Cheshire or Chester

Uses : Widespread. Desserts, snacks, Welsh Rarebit.

Origin : England (Cheshire).

Characteristics : Made from cow's milk. Fat (45%). Mild flavor. Natural brushed crust. The paste is uncooked and either white, blue or red in color. Blue Cheshire (Old Blue) is the oldest and the richest. Aged to perfection (2 years) it forms blue veins and is sold under the name of Blue Cheddar.

Related cheeses : Cheddar, Colby, Gloucester, etc.

Appearance : Comes in a cheesecloth-covered cylinder of from 12 to 14 pounds. Colored Cheshire comes in blocks of the same weight as well. Sold by desired weight. Also available in a minicheese of 1 lb.

How to choose it : Gives off a faint but pleasant odor. The crust should be solid, even, and only slightly waxy ; the cheese itself should be firm, oily, slightly supple, and homogeneous in spite of its natural granulation.

Be careful, however, of a cheese that is too granular.

How to enjoy it : With a Médoc, port, or beer. Also goes very well with tea and stalks of celery.

Historical background : Already well-known at the end of the XVIth century, during the reign of Elizabeth I.

REMARKS :

Chevrotin

Uses : Desserts, snacks.

Origin : France (Savoy).

Characteristics : Made from goat's milk (sometimes mixed with cow's milk). Fat (45%). Not so mild goaty flavor. Natural crust. Paste is pressed and uncooked.

Appearance : Comes in a flat wheel (1 pound and more). Sold in prepared 3 oz. portions.

How to choose it : Gives off no particular odor. The grey crust should be healthy, delicate, and rough textured ; the paste should be firm.

Beware of a cheese that is dried out or granular.

Colby

Uses : Desserts, with fruit, sandwiches.

Characteristics : A mild cheese of the Cheddar type. A semi-soft cheese that varies from a creamy white to orange in color, is elastic and pierced with small holes.

Comté or Gruyère de Comté

Uses : Very handy for desserts, snacks, canapés, or for cooking (gratins, fondues, croque-monsieur, doughnuts, onion soup).

Characteristics : Made from cow's milk. Fat (45%). Has a taste that is fruity and salty, and a bit stronger than that of Emmenthal. The crust is rough, sometimes moist. The paste is pressed, cooked and pierced with well-spread openings that are the size of a pea or, at the most, a cherry.

Related cheeses : Gruyère, Emmenthal, Beaufort.

Appearance : Comes in a convex-walled wheel of about 75 lbs. It is sold by desired weight or in prepared portions.

How to choose it : Gives off very little odor. The crust should be a bit rough, flat or slightly swollen ; the paste a pale ivory yellow, firm and a little on the supple side. Comté fans often prefer a paste that has small cracks in it. Moist holes take nothing away from the quality of the cheese. On the contrary, as is the case with all Gruyères, a Comté that is sweating out its salt will be much tastier.

Be careful of a crust that is too swollen and a paste that is elastic and that has holes which are too close together. The cheese will be either tasteless or sharp.

How to enjoy it : With a red Burgundy, a Côtes-duRhône, a Muscadet, or even with beer.

Historical background : Known since the XIIIth century.

Veal Cutlets Milanaise

Prepare and season each cutlet.

Mix equal parts of grated Comté and bread crumbs.

Dip the cutlets in flour, then in a whole beaten egg, and finally in the cheese-breadcrumb mixture.

Cook in butter at a low heat and serve immediately.

REMARKS :

Cottage Cheese (Canadian)

Uses : Used for desserts, snacks, main dishes.

Characteristics : Lean (10%). Mild, slightly acid and variable in flavor. This is a soft cheese, unripened, made from 2% skim milk, pasteurized ; a lactic fermenting agent and a small amount of rennin have been added. It takes 15 to 20 hours to make. Once cut and heated, the final product has a fat content of 10%.

There is also a 'cottage cheese that is even leaner, obtained from completely skimmed milk, that is cut but not heated. Some manufacturers differentiate between these two types of cottage cheese by the color of the packaging (red for the fat, blue for the lean).

Finally, there is also a cream cottage cheese with a base of 12% cream. Even though cut and heated, this cheese still has a fat content of only 4%. To this are sometimes added fruit, vegetables, herbs, or relish.

Cottage Cheese Dip

For about 1 cup of dip :

1 cup of strained cottage cheese
¼ cup of salad dressing
2 tbsp. of chopped green onion
A few drops of hot sauce

1 tsp. of lemon juice
Salt and pepper

Mix the ingredients and beat until a light consistency is achieved.

To obtain a rich cheese sauce, add the cheese only at the last minute and then heat until it melts, but no longer.

Cheese Pie

For 6 people :

1 cup of cottage cheese
1 lb. of ground beef
1 8'' pie shell
2 beaten eggs
2 tbsp. of flour
1 cup of chopped onions
¼ cup of finely chopped green pepper
2 tbsp. of melted butter
1 tsp. of Worcestershire sauce
Salt, pepper, and paprika

Sauté the onions and green pepper in butter (about 5 minutes).

Add the ground beef and allow to brown (4 to 5 minutes), add the flour and the seasoning (except for the paprika), and spread the mixture in the pie crust.

Mix the eggs and the cottage cheese together and pour over the meat.

Dust with paprika.

Brown at 350°F.for about 40 minutes.

REMARKS :

Coulommiers

Uses : Very handy, good for desserts, croquettes, canapés.

Origin : France (Ile-de-France and Champagne). Takes its name from the town of Coulommiers.

Characteristics : Made from cow's milk. Extra-fat (45 to 50%). Mild taste that brings to mind the flavor of sweet almonds when the cheese is ripened to perfection. White downy mould crust. The paste is soft, neither cooked nor pressed.

Related cheeses : Camembert, Brie.

Appearance : Comes in a round, 11 ounce box.

How to choose it : Its aroma should be pleasant and remi-

niscent of that of a Brie ; the crust should be very white and speckled with red ; the paste should be even, supple, and not runny.

Beware if there is too much white down or too much down on the crust.

How to enjoy it : With red wine, a Volnay, a Moulin-à-Vent, a Hermitage.

REMARKS :

Cream O Lack

Uses : Desserts, as a spread, grilled cheese sandwiches.

Characteristics : Semi-fat (27.5%). A mild cheese of the Cheddar type. The paste is a reddish orange and quite hard, but stretches easily when heated. Will keep from 2 to 3 months in an air-tight container.

How to enjoy it : With a red wine or beer.

REMARKS :

Crottin de Chavignol or Chavignol

Uses : Desserts, snacks.

Origin : France (Berry). From the village of Chavignol, its principal center of manufacture.

Characteristics : Made from goat's milk. Fat (45%). Nutty, mild flavor. Natural crust. Soft, uncooked paste.

Related cheese : Sancerre.

Appearance : Comes in a 2 ounce flattened ball.

How to choose it : Gives off a faint odor of goats. The crust is fine, bluish white, and speckled with reddish orange. The paste is firm and smooth.

Be careful of a cheese that is dried out and granular ; it might easily be too salty.

How to enjoy it : With a white Sancerre, or a Pinot.

NOTE : For those who are very fond of strong cheese, try some old Chavignol. Its size and weight are less as it has dried out. The crust turns dark grey or reddish brown, the paste hard and crumbly, and the flavor very strong and sharp.

REMARKS :

Danablu (Danish Blue)

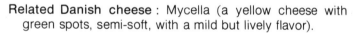

Uses : Desserts.

Origin : Denmark.

Characteristics : Made from cow's milk. Extra-fat (50%). Sharp flavor. Semi-soft paste that is very white and marbled with green and pale green.

Related Danish cheese : Mycella (a yellow cheese with green spots, semi-soft, with a mild but lively flavor).

Appearance : Comes in 5 to 6 pound foil-wrapped wheels. Sold by desired weight or in prepared portions.

How to enjoy it : With a Saint-Amour, a Romanèche, a Chateauneuf-du-Pape.

REMARKS :

Délice

Uses : Desserts. With various condiments, also good for sandwiches and snacks.

Origin : France (Brie). The name is a trademark.

Characteristics : Made from enriched milk. Triple-cream (75%). The flavor is mild, creamy, slightly nutty. Downy crust, soft paste.

Related cheeses : Boursault, Boursin, Brillat-Savarin.

Appearance : Comes in a 7 oz. wheel and in a 3½ oz. wheel (Demi-Délice).

How to choose it : Gives off a faint odor of cream and mushrooms. The crust is white and sprinkled with small reddish blotches. The paste is oily and not elastic.

Be careful of a crust that is dried out or that gives off an odor of phenol ; in other words, a cheese that is rancid.

How to enjoy it : With a Bouzy or Champagne.

REMARKS :

Délice (Canadian)

Uses : Desserts, canapés, sandwiches, appetizers, etc.

Characteristics : Triple-cream (75%). A soft cheese. Mild and creamy flavor. Good both when young and when old, it can satisfy all tastes.

Related cheeses : Boursault, Excelsior, Explorateur.

Appearance : Comes in a small 7 ounce wheel.

How to enjoy it : With Asti Spumante.

REMARKS :

Demi-Suisse

Uses : Desserts, snacks.

Type : French.

Characteristics : Extra-fat (50 to 55%). Prepared according to the methods used in France to make Petit-Suisse (see listing). It is an ideal cheese for desserts and children's snacks. Its special packaging insures good preservation and the paste, which is very homogeneous, spreads easily. Comes in 2 varieties : natural and with strawberries.

Appearance : Comes in a 6 ounce box that contains 6 portions.

Historical background : First made in Sutton, Quebec in 1967. Demi-Suisse with strawberries wasn't created until 1968.

REMARKS :

Double Gloucester

Origin : England.

Characteristics : Made from cow's milk. The cheese is light in color, rich, smooth, and pierced with small openings, and has a flavor reminiscent of Cheddar.

Appearance : Comes in a plastic-wrapped wheel that weighs about 8 lbs. Also comes in a 1 pound mini-cheese.

How to enjoy it : With a red wine or beer.

Ducs de Bourgogne

Uses : Quite handy for desserts.

Origin : France (Burgundy).

Characteristics : Made from cow's milk. Extra-fat (50%). Mild flavor. Downy crust. Soft paste.

Appearance : Comes in a small 4 ounce cylinder packed in a labelled carton.

How to choose it : Impossible. Trust your luck.

How to enjoy it : With a rosé or a white wine, a Chablis.

Edam

Uses : Very versatile. Good for lunches, desserts, snacks, toast, canapés, etc.

Origin : Holland. Comes from the small port city of Edam, not far from Amsterdam. There are also French and German Edams.

Characteristics : Made from cow's milk. Fat (40%). The flavor is fresh, mild, nutty, and sometimes a bit salty. This last becomes more pronounced with age. Has a paraffined crust that is dyed red or yellow. The paste is semi-soft, pressed, uncooked, orange in color, and either without holes or with a few very small ones.

Related cheeses : Mimolette, Gouda.

Appearance : Comes in a 4 pound ball (Tête de Maure) or in one that weighs 2 pounds (Baby Edam). Also in a 5 pound loaf. It is sold by desired weight or in prepared packages.

How to choose it : Gives off a faint milky odor. It should either be very round or very geometrical in shape ; the crust smooth ; the paste supple and elastic. Beware of a cheese with holes that are too large, but this only happens occasionally.

How to enjoy it : With a light white wine, a red Beaujolais, a Muscadet, or a strong beer. Cut into small cubes and dipped in celery salt, it accompanies an appetizer very well.

Fricandelles

5¼ oz. of Edam
4½ oz. of ground pork
4½ oz. of ground veal
3 eggs
2 tbsp. of milk
1 rusk
1¾ oz. of butter
Breadcrumbs
Nutmeg
Salt and pepper
Tomato sauce
Chopped pickles

Mix the meat, the eggs and the crumbled rusk. Season.

Cut the Edam into tiny cubes and mix it with the above.

Shape into small balls (Fricandelles).

Dip into an egg beaten with the milk and roll in bread-crumbs.

Let stand a moment and then repeat this last operation.

Brown the fricandelles in butter (all sides to obtain a crust).

Cook over a very low heat for 20 minutes.

Serve covered with tomato sauce and garnished with the chopped pickles.

REMARKS :

Emmental or Emmenthal

Uses : Very handy for desserts, sandwiches, salads, sauces, fondues.

Origin : Switzerland. Takes its name from the town of Emmenthal in Berne Canton. It can be recognized by the word " Switzerland " stamped on the crust.

There are also Emmenthals made in Canada (natural Swiss), Holland, France (made in Burgundy and Savoy), Germany, Austria, Denmark, and Norway (Jarlsberg). There are process Emmenthal spreads as well.

Characteristics : Made from cow's milk. Fat (43%). It is a Gruyère with holes at least as large as cherries. It has a mild, nutty and sweet flavor, the mildest of all the Gruyères. The crust is brushed and greased, hard dry, and golden in color. The paste is hard, pressed, and cooked.

Related cheeses : Gruyère, Comté, Beaufort.

Appearance : Comes in a swollen wheel that can weigh up to 100 lbs. It is sold by desired weight and in prepared slices of 6 oz. or more.

Grated : in an 8 oz. bag.

Dutch Emmenthal (Baby Swiss) : 8 oz.

How to choose it : The crust should be healthy and smooth ; the odor faintly milky ; the paste firm, not too elastic, and the color of yellow ivory. The holes are spherical, well spaced, neither too large nor too small.

Beware of a crust that is overly swollen, and of a paste that is too elastic, wrinkled, or cracked. Holes that are too large or oval indicate a defective fermentation. The cheese will either be sharp or without flavor.

Some people prefer a slightly cracked paste.

How to enjoy it : With red Burgundy, Muscadet, or beer.

Onion Soup Parisian Style

For each person :

3½ oz. of grated Emmenthal
1 or 2 onions, depending on their size
A handful of croutons browned in butter
1 bowl of bouillon
Butter
Pepper, salt, and nutmeg

Cut the onions into thin circles, brown them in the butter, add the bouillon and leave to simmer over a low heat.

Place the croutons in a small earthenware bowl, and add a layer of Emmenthal.

Add the bouillon, sprinkle again with the cheese, and brown in the oven.

Potato Gnocchi

For four persons :

Cook 2½ lbs. of potatoes. Be careful not to overcook.

Drain and let cool.

Mash well and mix in 3 egg yolks with salt, pepper, and nutmeg.

Allow the paste to stand for one hour.

With hands that are well-floured, shape small balls and then cook them for five minutes in salted water.

Place the gnocchi in a casserole . Dot with butter, sprinkle lightly with Emmenthal and brown for ten minutes in a very hot oven.

REMARKS :

Epoisses

Uses : Desserts.

Origin : France (Burgundy). Takes its name from the village where it is made.

Characteristics : Made from cow's milk. Fat (45%). Strong, earthy flavor. Washed crust. Soft paste washed with two-year-old Burgundy pulp.

Appearance : Comes in a round 9 oz. box. Also in a 5 oz. box under the name of Petit Epoisses.

How to choose it : Gives off a pleasant and penetrating odor. The orange-red crust should be smooth and shiny. The paste should be butter yellow, soft and supple.

Beware of a paste that is grey and granular. The cheese will be sharp.

How to enjoy it : With a Burgundy, a Nuits St-Georges, a Beaune, or black coffee.

Historical background : The favourite cheese of Napoleon Bonaparte.

Ermite (Canadian Blue)

Uses : Desserts (alone or with fruit), canapés, salads, salad dressing.

Origin : The Benedictine Monastery of St-Benoît-du-Lac (Quebec).

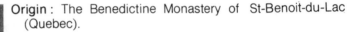

Characteristics : Extra-fat (48%). This is a Blue that is less salty than Roquefort and not as creamy as Danish Blue. The paste,which is creamy white and veined with blue, is semi-soft and crumbly. Sharp, peppery flavor.

Appearance : Comes in 4 or 7 oz. portions.

How to enjoy it : With a red wine, a Beaujolais or a Chianti.

Historical background : The first blue cheese (Bleu de Laqueuille) was manufactured in 1854 by Antoine Roussel-Laqueuille (Puy-de-Dôme, France).

Blue Salad Dressing

Liven up the flavor of a vinaigrette or a mayonnaise by adding crumbled blue cheese.

Esrom

Uses : Handy for desserts.

Origin : Denmark.

Characteristics : Made from cow's milk. Fat (45%). Mild flavor. Has a thin crust that is the color of a dead leaf. The paste is golden yellow.

Appearance : Comes foil-wrapped in blocks of 3 lbs., 1 lb. and in prepared portions of 8 oz.

How to enjoy it : With a Volnay.

REMARKS :

Fondue au Raisin (or Fondue au Marc)

Uses : Handy for desserts, snacks, toast, canapés.

Origin : France (Savoy). Takes its name from the nature of its paste and its appearance.

Characteristics : Made from cow's milk. Fat (45%). Mild flavor. Artificial crust made from grilled grape seeds. The yellow paste is a high quality French Gruyère, processed but not aged.

Related cheese : None.

How to choose it : Without hesitation.
  Be careful of a dry and cracked paste that is due to poor preservation.

How to enjoy it : With a fruity rosé or Arbois.

REMARKS :

Fontina

Uses : Handy for desserts, snacks, fondues. When old and grated, is used as a cooking condiment.

Origin : Italy (Piedmont). Takes its name from the rich oily nature of its paste. One can also find Fontinas made in Canada as well as in Denmark.

Characteristics : Made from cow's milk. Extra-fat (45 to 50%). The flavor is mild, delicate, and perfumed. The crust is washed, thin, and compact. The paste is pressed, uncooked, and pierced with a few holes.

Related cheese : Fontal.

Appearance : Comes in a flat, concave-sided wheel of from 15 to 25 lbs. Sold by desired weight.

How to choose it : Gives off an agreeable odor. The crust must be thin, and not overly rough ; the paste a pale yellow, supple, and with very small holes.

Beware of a paste that is sandy, swollen or with holes that are too large.

How to enjoy it : With a light red wine, a Valpolicella, a Bouzy.

Historical background : As far back as the thirteenth century, it was served at the table of the Dukes of Savoy.

REMARKS :

Fourme d'Ambert

Uses : Handy for desserts and snacks.

Origin : France (Auvergne).

Characteristics : Made from cow's milk. Fat (45%). Very pronounced, slightly bitter flavor. Dry crust with mould that is a result of the soaking which used to take place in natural caves.

How to choose it : Gives off a faint odor of caves. The dark grey crust must be healthy with white, light yellow and bright red mould. The paste, speckled with blue should be firm and homogeneous.

Be careful of a crust that is sticky, thick or cracked, as well as of a paste that is granular. There is a risk that the cheese will be too bitter.

How to enjoy it : With à Beaujolais, a Tavel, a Châteauneuf-du-Pape.

REMARKS :

Fromaggini

Uses : Mostly grated, on spaghetti.

Type : Italian.

Characteristics : Made from milk that is pasteurized and partially skimmed (1 or 2%).

Appearance : Comes in a small flat wheel.

REMARKS :

Gjetost (pronounced " Yetost ")

Uses : Desserts, snacks.

Origin : Norway.

Characteristics : Made from a mixture of cow's and goat's milk or from goat's milk alone. Fat (45%). A typically Norwegian cheese. Slightly sweet flavor. The paste is a smooth reddish brown.

Appearance : Ski Queen Gjetost (cow's and goat's milk) : comes in square blocks of 9 lbs., 1 lb., 8 oz.
Ekte Gjetost (pure goat's milk) : 2 lbs., 1 lb.

How to enjoy it : With a white wine or a dry rosé. Try it also with hot chocolate and buttered raisin bread.

REMARKS :

Goat's Milk Cheese and Ste-Maure

Uses : Desserts, snacks, cocktail canapés.

Characteristics : Extra-fat (58%). Made from fresh goat's milk. Sold fresh or aged.

Appearance : In a small 4 oz. pot — the paste is fresh and soft and has a neutral flavor. In a small wheel of 6 oz. (natural cheese, aged, with a mouldy crust and a flavor typical of goat's milk cheese). In a 5 oz. log, under the name " *Ste-Maure* " (same characteristics and flavor as the former, only the shape is different).

How to enjoy it : With a dry wine, Vouvray, Muscadet.

Historical background : First made in Sutton, Quebec, in 1972, the rarity of goat's milk in Canada did not permit the creation of such a cheese until this recently.

Gorgonzola (Italian Blue)

Uses : Very handy. Good for desserts.

Origin : Italy (Lombardy). Takes its name from the village where it was first created.

Characteristics : Made from cow's milk. Extra-fat (48%). The flavor is mild, medium, or strong and sharp depending on the age. Natural crust, that is scraped, washed and oiled. The paste is soft with blue or green veins similar to those in Roquefort.

Related cheeses : Bleu de Bresse, Gorgone.

Appearance : Comes in a labelled, foil-wrapped wheel of 13 to 26 lbs. Sold by desired weight.

How to choose it : Gives off a rather strong odor. The reddish grey crust should be quite smooth ; the paste, white or straw colored, should be very tender, almost runny.

Beware of a paste that is hard and that has too few veins. The cheese risks being too sharp.

How to enjoy it : With a red wine : Bordeaux, Burgundy, Côtes-du-Rhône.

Gouda

Uses : Very handy. Desserts (by itself or with fresh fruit), canapés, sandwiches, sauces, salads, etc.

Origin : Holland (guaranteed by the label " Volvet "). Takes its name from the small river port from which it is exported. There are also Goudas made in Canada, France, Denmark, and Finland (Kartano).

Characteristics : Made from cow's milk. Extra-fat (48%). The flavor is mild, nutty and silghtly acid. The crust is dyed red and paraffined. The paste is semi-soft, pressed, uncooked, and either natural or spiced.

Related cheeses : Edam (less fat : 40%), Leyde, Norbo, Mimolette.

Appearance : Comes in a very convex-sided wheel of 7 to 11 lbs. ; also available in a 20 lb. size. Sold by desired weight and in Baby Goudas of 10, 12, and 14 oz. It is sold young, medium, or old

Dutch Process Gouda : 8 oz.

French Gouda : 7 oz.

Smoked French Gouda (Fumagou) : 8 oz.

How to choose it : Gives off no special odor. The crust should be smooth and gleaming ; the paste smooth, fairly homogeneous, firm, almost elastic and dotted with small holes.

Be careful of a paste that is too dry and crumbly. The cheese will be sharp.

How to enjoy it : With a Beaujolais, a Médoc, a red Graves, or beer.

Gouda Doughnuts

To make 15 doughnuts :

10½ oz. of medium Gouda

5¼ oz. of flour
2¾ oz. of butter
1 egg
1 tbsp. of milk
3 tbsp. of beer
1 tsp. of sugar
1 pinch of salt

Place the flour on a pastry board, add the sugar and the salt and mix in the butter.

Work the beer into the dough.

Roll out the dough to a thickness of ¼ inch, fold in four and roll again to a thickness of 1/10 inch.

Cut the dough into squares that are 4 inches on a side.

Cut the Gouda into slices ¼ inch thick, then into squares 1½ inches on a side.

Dip the pieces of cheese in the egg that has been beaten and diluted with the milk before wrapping them in the squares of dough.

Moisten the edges with beaten egg and drop the doughnuts into hot frying oil. Serve hot with tomato sauce.

REMARKS :

Gouda (Canadian)

Uses : Desserts (by itself or with fresh fruit), sandwiches, sauces, salads.

Type : Dutch.

Characteristics : Extra-fat (48%). Mild, nutty, slightly acid flavor. The crust is covered with red paraffin. The paste is semi-soft, smooth, almost elastic. A good Gouda takes at least 6 months to become luscious and light, and to acquire its buttery taste.

Appearance : Comes in a 10-ounce wheel.

How to enjoy it : With a red wine (preferably sweet if the Gouda is served as a dessert), or with beer.

REMARKS :

Gournay

Uses : Handy for desserts.

Origin : France (the Bray country of Normandy). Takes its name from the village where it was first made. There is also a Canadian-made Gournay.

Characteristics : Made from cow's milk. Fat (45%). Mild flavor that is a bit on the salty and acid side. Downy crust. Soft, uncooked paste.

Related cheeses : Neufchâtel, Bondon.

Appearance : Comes in a small, round, 3 oz. box. Canadian Gournay, which comes in a 4 oz. square, is also available seasoned, either with herbs, pimento and celery, or onions.

How to choose it : Gives off a faint odor of milk and of mould. The crust should be white and downy ; the paste smooth and supple.

Beware of a granular paste which can easily be too salty.

How to enjoy it : With a light red wine, a Bourgueil, a Chinon, a Bouzy.

Historical background : One of the oldest cheeses of upper Normandy.

REMARKS :

Grain Cheese

This is a cheese curd obtained by the coagulation of the insoluble elements of the milk.

Instead of being pressed in moulds, as is the case for an ordinary cheese, the grains of curd are packed, labelled, and delivered to the consumer under the name of *Grain Cheese.*

This type of cheese has the same fat content as its corresponding pressed cheese (Cheddar or other).

REMARKS :

Gruyère

Uses : A very versatile cheese. Good for snacks, desserts, cooking (fondues, cheese steaks, gratins, salads, seasoning).

Origin : Switzerland. Comes from the region of Gruyère (Friburg Canton). Guaranteed by the word " Switzerland " on the label. One can also find Canadian, Austrian, Danish, and American Gruyères. The French Gruyères each have their own particular name (Emmenthal, Comté, Beaufort).

Characteristics : Made from cow's milk. Fat (45%). Mild, nutty, slightly salty flavor. Canadian Gruyère is slightly sharper. Brushed crust. The paste is pressed, cooked, and is pierced with small holes.

Appearance : Comes in a slightly convex-sided flat wheel of 60 to 80 lbs. ; in points of 5 lbs. and more. It is sold by desired weight or in prepared portions.

How to choose it : Gives off a rather pleasant odor. The crust should be healthy and not very rough ; the paste should be ivory yellow in color and firm, but should still have some give when pressed by the finger. The holes are rare and small, about the size of a pea or a bit larger.

Beware if small cracks form beneath the crust. A granular paste may prove to be sharp, though some people prefer it this way.

How to enjoy it : With a white, fruity wine, a Mâcon, an Arbois rosé, a Muscadet, or beer.

Historical background : Already well-known in the twelfth century and certainly much older.

Swiss Fondue

To serve four :

1 cup of grated Gruyère
1 cup of grated Emmenthal
1 cup of dry white wine
1 small clove of garlic, crushed
1 ½ tbsp. of flour
½ tsp. of dry mustard
½ tsp. of salt
½ tsp. of pepper
French bread cut into 1-inch cubes.

Heat the wine and garlic in a fondu dish until the wine begins to boil.

Mix the two cheeses with the rest of the ingredients.

Add to the wine a bit at a time (tablespoon by tablespoon) while stirring constantly.

Cook only until all the cheese is melted, since overcooking will make it harden.

Serve in the fondue dish under which a sufficient amount of heat must be maintained.

To eat, skewer cubes of bread on a fork and dip them in the Swiss Fondue.

REMARKS :

Gruyère (Canadian)

Uses : Desserts, snacks, cooking (fondues, gratins, salads, seasoning, etc.).

Type : Swiss.

Characteristics : Extra-fat (48%). The flavor is salty and nutty, similar to the Swiss product, but sharper. Hard crust ; the paste is pale yellow, firm and smooth, pierced with small holes.

Appearance : Comes in blocks and slices of various weights.

How to enjoy it : With a white wine or beer.

Cheese Soufflé

For 6 persons :

1 pint of milk
Butter
Flour
2 tbsp. of starch
6 eggs
3½ oz. of Gruyère
Salt
Fresh ground pepper

For best results, 2 soufflé dishes are required.

Boil the pint of milk with a coffee spoon of salt and a pinch of fresh ground pepper.

In a large pot, melt 3½ oz. of butter and add 3½ oz. of flour and 2 tbsp. of starch that have been sifted together.

Remove from the heat and mix together using a mixing whip.

Pour in the boiling milk and put the pot back on the heat, stirring continuously with the whip. Remove from the heat as soon as the boiling point is reached.

One minute later, add 6 egg yolks, 2 at a time, making sure that they are perfectly blended in each time.

Add 3½ oz. of Gruyère that has been cut into very fine strips.

Beat the 6 egg whites until very stiff and add them gently without stirring.

Fill to the brim the two soufflé dishes that have been generously buttered right to the top.

Place in the oven which has been preheated to 390°F.

Allow to cook for 25 minutes, but after a quarter of an hour keep a close eye on the color.

If necessary, cover with absorbent paper.

Eggs Dariole

For 6 persons :

3 tbsp. of Gruyère
6 eggs
2 oz. of fresh cream
6 slices of crusty bread, toasted
Tomato sauce.

6 small dariole cups are required.

Butter the cups and sprinkle them with grated Gruyère (about 1 tablespoon among the 6).

Beat 6 medium-size eggs with a good 2 oz. of thick, fresh cream and 2 tbsp. of grated Gruyère.

Add salt and pepper and pour the mixture into the cups, filling them ¾ full.

Place the covered cups in boiling water halfway up the sides of the cups and allow to cook for about 20 minutes.

Remove the cups as soon as the mixture rises to the lip of the cups and is firm to the touch.

Turn out the darioles onto 6 slices of toasted crusty bread previously browned in oil and butter (equal amounts).

Serve with a spicy and aromatic tomato sauce.

REMARKS :

Havarti

Uses : Handy for desserts.

Origin : Denmark.

Characteristics : Made from cow's milk. Fat (45%). A slightly tart flavor that becomes sharp with age. The paste is yellow, almost firm, either natural or spiced, and pierced with numerous holes.

Appearance : Comes in a 10 lb. foil-wrapped cylinder. Sold by desired weight.

How to enjoy it : With a Beaujolais.

REMARKS :

Isle d'Orléans Cheeses (Quebec)

Fromage de l'Isle :

Made from rich milk, this cheese with a very soft white paste is excellent for spreading. It is very similar to the Oka of yesteryear when it was sold less aged. Goes very well with a very dry red wine.

Fromage Sec :

Unpasteurized, which might be of interest to those who like natural foods, it is comparable to a mild unripened Cheddar. The perfect health of the cattle and the care surrounding its manufacture assure the buyer of its hygienic qualities. Sold fresh on the farm, it is only after six weeks' aging that it is sold commercially. To appreciate it at its best, serve it slightly warm. It requires a very dry red wine.

A greatly appreciated local craft, the cheeses of the Isle d'Orléans are manufactured from mid-November to the end of April according to very old recipes handed down from generation to generation. Their sale, which is strictly local, is limited to Quebec City. They come in 8 oz. portions.

REMARKS :

Jarlsberg

Uses : Desserts, snacks, cooking.

Origin : Norway.

Characteristics : Made from cow's milk. It is a fat cheese (45%) that falls between Gouda and Emmenthal. The flavor is mild and nutty. The rich, semi-soft paste with large holes is protected by yellow wax.

Appearance : Comes in a 20 lb. wheel and in a 13 lb. block without crust. Sold by desired weight.

How to enjoy it : With a dry white wine (Rhine, Moselle) or a light red (Beaujolais, Médoc, Chianti).

Jarlsberg Soufflé

To serve 4 persons :

8 oz. (approx.) of diced Jarlsberg
2 oz. of butter
1½ oz. of unleavened flour
1 pint of milk (approx.)
3 eggs (yolks and whites separated)
2 tbsp. of grated cheese (Norbo, Norvegia, or Cheddar)
Salt

Prepare a thick Béchamel with the butter, the flour, and the milk.

Allow to cool slightly.

Mix the diced Jarlsberg with the egg yolks.

Beat the egg whites until stiff and add them carefully.

Pour the mixture into a buttered dish.

Sprinkle with grated cheese and place in the oven at 300°F. for 30 to 40 minutes.

Serve with French bread and butter.

Pizza Nordica

To serve 4 or 5 persons :

8 oz. of grated Jarlsberg
3 oz. of butter
4 oz. (approx.) of flour
1 coffee spoon of unleavened flour
2 cups of water
2 or 3 sliced tomatoes (or ketchup)
8 anchovy fillets
6 stuffed olives or 1 tbsp. of sliced pimento
1 coffee spoon of salt

Melt the butter in a frying pan.

Mix the two kinds of flour, the salt, water, and butter to make a dough.

Spread the dough in the bottom of a frying pan and cook over a high heat until the bottom of the crust is browned.

Remove from the heat and turn the dough over with a spatula or a knife.

Cover with slices of tomatoes (or ketchup) and anchovies.

Sprinkle with the Jarlsberg, garnish with olives or pimento.

Place the pan back on the stove and brown the underside of the pizza.

Wait until the cheese has melted and then serve very hot.

Lancashire

Origin : England.

Characteristics : Made from cow's milk. White, with a granular paste pierced with openings. The flavor is mild, medium, or sharp, depending on the degree of aging.

Appearance : Comes in a plastic-wrapped wheel of about 8 lbs. Also comes in a 1 lb. minicheese.

How to enjoy it : With a red wine or with beer.

Welsh Rarebit

For 4 persons :

Beat 3½ oz. of grated Cheshire or Lancashire with 5 tablespoons of beer and 1 of mustard.

Spread the mixture over 4 slices of buttered toast and cook in a lightly-greased covered frying pan.

Leicester

Origin : England.

Characteristics : Made from cow's milk. The light reddish paste, pierced with openings, has a very aromatic flavor that is more or less accentuated according to the age of the cheese.

Appearance : Comes in a plastic-wrapped wheel of 7 to 8 lbs. It is sold by desired weight.

How to enjoy it : With a light red wine, Saint-Emilion. With walnuts or grapes.

REMARKS :

Leyde

Uses : Quite versatile. Lunches, desserts, snacks.

Origin : Holland (Zuid Holland). Takes its name from the city of Leyde which was once the place where it was sold.

Characteristics : Made from cow's milk. Fat (40%). Mild, aromatic flavor. Washed, brushed crust. The paste is semi-soft, pressed, heated, and sprinkled with cumin seeds.

Related cheeses : Edam, Gouda, Mimolette.

Appearance : Comes in a labelled, slightly convex-walled wheel of from 11 to 22 lbs. It is sold by desired weight and in prepared portions.

How to choose it : Gives off little odor. The greyish yellow crust should be delicate and smooth ; the paste firm and supple. Faults are rarely to be seen.

How to enjoy it : With a Beaujolais or with beer.

REMARKS :

Limburger

Uses : Desserts, preferably with rye bread.

Origin : Belgium and Holland (the province of Limburg in each country). Limburgers made in Canada and in Germany are also available.

Characteristics : Made from cow's milk. Semi-fat (30 to 40%) or extra-fat (48%). Very strong, sharp flavor. Washed crust. Soft, uncooked paste.

Related cheeses : Hervé, Remoudou, Maroilles.

Appearance : Comes in a square-ended rectangular block of about 1½ lbs. Sold by desired weight.

How to choose it : Gives off a powerful, but pleasant, odor. The crust, which is brick red or greyish brown should be delicate and smooth ; the paste should be creamy white or yellow, depending on the origin of the cheese. It should be supple, smooth, and dotted with small, irregular holes.

Be careful of a crust that is wrinkled ; of a paste that is firm and granular. The cheese may have a taste of ammonia.

How to enjoy it : With a good red wine, a Chateauneuf-du-Pape.

Historical background : It was probably created by the monks of one of the numerous monasteries that existed in Limburg in the Middle Ages.

REMARKS :

Livarot

Uses : Quite handy. Good for desserts, snacks.

Origin : France (Normandy). Named after the small town of Livarot.

Characteristics : Made from cow's milk. Fat (40 to 45%). Rather strong flavor. Washed crust. Soft, very slightly salted, uncooked paste.

Related cheese : Pont-l'Évêque.

Appearance : Comes in a round 5 oz. box.

How to choose it : Normally, its odor is strong. The crust should be even, smooth, shiny, going from light brown to dark brown ; the paste fine, elastic, and without holes. Beware of a rotten smell, of a crust that is dried out or sticky, of a rough or holey poaste. A good Livarot should not be runny.

How to enjoy it : With a Pomerol, a Côtes-du-Rhône, cider, or even a small glass of Calvados.

Historical background : One of the oldest of Norman cheeses, it was originally made by monks and probably was called Angelot.

REMARKS :

Maroilles

Uses : Quite handy. Desserts, snacks, cheese pie.

Origin : France (Hainault, Flanders). Named after the small town of Maroilles.

Characteristics : Made from cow's milk. Extra-fat (45 to 50%). Very pronounced earthy flavor. Washed, un-mouldy crust. The paste is white, mild, soft, and per-fumed.

Appearance : Comes in a labelled block of about 2 lbs. and in one of 5 oz. under the name of Quart de Ma-roilles.

How to choose it : Gives off a strong odor. The reddish brown crust should be shiny and smooth ; the paste supple.

Beware of a smell of ammonia, a crust that is too dried out, or a chalky paste.

How to enjoy it : With a Pommard, a Nuits-St-Georges, a Château-Lafitte, or beer.

Historical background : Created in the Xth century by a monk of the Abbey of Maroilles, where the body of Saint Hubert, bishop of Tongres in the VIIIth century and the patron saint of hunters, was buried. Originally called '' craquegnon '' or '' Merveille de Maroilles '', it was a favorite of several kings of France : Philip-Augustus, Saint-Louis, Charles VI, Francis 1, Henry IV, and of the Holy Roman Emperor, Charles V.

REMARKS :

Mimolette or Boule de Lille or Vieux Lille

Uses : Quite versatile. Desserts, snacks, canapés, seasoning (grated).

Origin : France (Flanders). True Mimolette is Dutch in origin.

Characteristics : Made from cow's milk. Fat (45%). Mild, nutty flavor. Natural brushed crust. The paste is pressed, uncooked, and colored.

Related cheeses : Edam, Gouda.

Appearance : With a guarantee label, in a slightly flattened ball weighing 4 lbs. Sold by desired weight and in prepared portions.

How to choose it : Gives off a faint, pleasant odor. The grey crust must be delicate and even; the orange-colored paste, oily and firm.

Beware of a fissured crust, or of a paste with holes. The cheese may be either sharp or rancid.

How to enjoy it : With an apéritif wine (port, Madeira, Banyuls), or a regular wine (red Burgundy, Arbois, Beaujolais).

Historical background : The favorite cheese of General de Gaulle.

Sandwiches

7 oz. of Mimolette
3½ oz. of cream cheese
2 tbsp. of chopped walnuts
Chopped chives, salt, and pepper

Crush and grind all the ingredients.

Spread on slices of bread that can then be cut into small triangles.

Canapés or Toast

1 whole Mimolette
Port or Madeira

Open the top of the cheese and take out the paste in little balls, using a pastry tool.

Sprinkle lightly with port or Madeira and allow to steep for a week or two.

Serve as is on toast or crushed for canapés.

REMARKS :

Montasio

Uses : Handy for desserts, snacks. Old and grated : as a cooking condiment.

Origin : Italy (Venice). Takes its name from the fields of a convent where the herds grazed when it was still made from ewe's milk (XIIIth century). There is also a Canadian-made Montasio.

Characteristics : Made from cow's milk. Semi-fat (30%). Mild, nutty flavor when the cheese is young. It becomes strong, rancid, and sharp with age. Brushed crust. The paste is pressed, uncooked, and has small holes scattered throughout.

Appearance : Comes in a slightly convex-sided wheel of 13 lbs. and more. Sold by desired weight.

How to choose it : Gives off no particular odor. The crust, which is yellow ochre or grey, should be slightly rough ; the paste both firm and supple. If it is hard and brittle, it is an old cheese.

How to enjoy it : Young — with a Beaujolais. Old — with a Chateauneuf-du-Pape.

REMARKS :

Montrachet

Uses : Desserts.

Origin : France (Burgundy). From the name of a Burgundian vineyard famous for its white wines.

Characteristics : Made from goat's milk. Fat (45%). Mild, creamy flavor. The crust is barely formed. The paste is soft and uncooked. Imported by air.

Related cheeses : All semi-fresh goat cheeses.

Appearance : Comes in a small 5 oz. cylinder wrapped in vine or chestnut leaves.

How to choose it : Gives off a faint, goaty odor. The crust should be healthy looking and bluish ; the paste supple.

Be careful of a paste that is crumbly. The cheese may be sharp.

How to enjoy it : With a very dry white wine, a Beaujolais.

REMARKS :

Morbier

Uses : Quite handy for desserts and snacks.

Origin : France (Franche-Comté). Named after the village of Morbier where it is made.

Characteristics : Made from cow's milk. Fat (45%). The flavor is not very pronounced. Natural brushed crust. The paste is pressed, uncooked, and has a horizontal black stripe through the middle.

Appearance : Comes in a wheel of 10 to 12 lbs. Sold by desired weight.

How to choose it : Gives off a faint lactic odor. The crust should be light grey ; the paste both firm and supple.

Be careful of a paste that is hard and inflexible. The cheese risks being bitter.

How to enjoy it : With a Beaujolais, a red Burgundy, a Côtes-du-Rhône.

REMARKS :

Mozzarella (Pizza Cheese)

Uses : Snacks, sandwiches, pizza, lasagna.

Origin : Italy (Campania). See also Mozzarella (Canadian).

Characteristics : Made from cow's milk or from the milk of oxen. Semi-fat (30%) or fat (44%). Mild, creamy, slightly acid flavor. No crust. The paste is without mould, pressed and strained, and neither cooked nor aged.

Appearance : Variable : comes in the shape of a sphere, a loaf, or a drawstring purse. Weight varies from 3 oz. to 2½ lbs.

How to choose it : Gives off an odor that is quite milky. The paste is spotlessly white and elastic.

Beware of a yellowish paste. The cheese is too old.

How to enjoy it : With a white wine or a rosé, preferably Italian.

Mozzarella (Canadian)

Uses : Snacks, sandwiches, pizza, lasagna, baked macaroni, Béchamel sauce.

Type : Italian.

Characteristics : Made from whole milk that is pasteurized and partially skimmed. Made both by hand and by automated processes. Very mild flavor. No crust. The paste is a creamy white, unaged, semi-soft, and has a plastic texture. Similar to the French cheese, Demi-Sel. Keeps for up to 2 months.

Appearance : Comes in a small 5 lb. ball and is also sold by desired weight.

How to enjoy it : With a red or rosé wine (Chianti, etc.)

Minipizza

Garnish squares or rounds of bread with chili sauce.

Sprinkle with salt, and top with a thin slice of Mozzarella, anchovies, olives or a bit of pepperoni.

Broil for 2 minutes to allow the cheese to melt.

Lasagna with Tomato Sauce

(For 8 people)

For the Lasagna :

1 lb. of thinly-sliced Mozzarella
½ cup of grated Parmesan
8 oz. of lasagna noodles
1 lb. of cottage cheese
1 beaten egg
1 tbsp. of chopped parsley
Salt and pepper

Cook the noodles in boiling salted water (10 cups of water, 2 tsp. of salt) until tender, which takes about 10 minutes. Then drain.

Mix the cottage cheese, beaten egg, salt, and pepper.

Pour a bit of tomato sauce into a greased baking dish that is 13 x 8 x 2 inches.

Add alternating layers of half of the noodles, the cottage cheese and egg mixture, Mozzarella, and tomato sauce.

Repeat in the same order, but save a bit of Mozzarella.

Finally, sprinkle with Parmesan and garnish with thin strips of Mozzarella.

Cook at 350° F for about 35 minutes.

Sprinkle with chopped parsley and let stand for a quarter of an hour.

For the Tomato Sauce :
1 28-oz. can of tomatoes
1 5-oz. can of tomato paste
2 tbsp. of oil
1 cup of chopped onions
½ cup of diced celery
½ cup of diced green pepper
2 cloves of garlic, crushed
1 tbsp. of chopped parsley
¼ tsp. of crushed chili peppers
½ tsp. of oregano
2 tsp. of sugar
1 ½ tsp. of salt
1 pinch of pepper

Sauté the onions, green pepper, celery, and garlic in oil until the onions become transparent (about 5 minutes).

Add the rest of the ingredients, cover, and let simmer for about 2 hours, stirring from time to time.

REMARKS :

Munster

Uses : Quite handy for desserts, snacks, sandwiches.

Origin : France (Alsace). Named after the town of Munster (a contraction of the word monastery).

Characteristics : Made from cow's milk. Extra-fat (45 to 50%). A pleasant flavor that is either pronounced or very pronounced. A washed crust that is without mould. The paste is soft, uncooked, and slightly salty. It is also made seasoned with cumin.

123

Related cheeses : Canadian Brick, Danish Munster, Epoisses, Géromé.

Appearance : Comes in a round, labelled box of 8 oz. and of 4 oz. under the name of Baby Munster.

How to choose it : Gives off a strong and penetrating odor. The crust, which is pale red or brownish, should be smooth ; the paste should be a creamy yellow, soft, rich, and dotted with small holes.

Be careful of a paste that is dried out or crumbly.

How to enjoy it : With a Alsatian Pinot Rouge, a Gewürztraminer, a Corton, a Beaujolais, a Côtes-du-Rhône.

Historical background : Created by monks in the VIIth century. The original methods of manufacture have been carefully preserved.

REMARKS :

Murol

Uses : Handy for desserts, snacks, tid-bits.

Origin : France (Auvergne). Named after the village of Murol where it is made.

Characteristics : Made from the milk of mountain cattle. Fat (45%). Mild flavor. Washed crust. The paste is pressed and uncooked.

Related cheeses : Saint-Paulin, Saint-Nectaire, Oka, Anfrom.

Appearance : Comes in a small 12 oz. wheel.

How to choose it : Gives off no special odor. The pinkish crust and the paste must both be flexible.

Be careful of dried-out crust and a hard paste.

Neufchâtel (or Bonde, Bondon, Bondard)

Uses : Good for desserts and snacks.

Origin : France (Normandy). From the small village of Neufchâtel-en-Bray, the principal cheese market of the region.

Characteristics : Made from cow's milk. Fat or extra-fat (45 to 48%). Mild delectable flavor. Downy crust. The paste is soft and uncooked.

Related cheeses : Gournay, Malakof.

Appearance : Very diverse, Bondon is round, but Neufchâtel is also available in squares, bricks, and heart shapes. The average weight is 3½ oz.

How to choose it : Gives off a faint fungus smell, the crust should be downy, and very faintly tinged with red ; the paste should be rich, smooth, and homogeneous.

Be careful of a crust that is dried out or a paste that is granular. The cheese may be too salty.

How to enjoy it : With a Côtes-du-Rhône, a Jurançon, a Mouton-Cadet.

Historical background : Supposedly the ancestor of all Norman cheeses.

Nökkelost (or Noökkel)

Uses : Desserts, sandwiches, cocktail tid-bits, appetizers, cooking.

Origin : Norway.

Characteristics : Made from cow's milk. Semi-fat (30%) or fat (45%). The flavor is fresh, spicy, and perfumed. Has no crust. The paste is spiced with cumin seeds and cloves, and is covered with red wax.

Appearance : Comes in wheels of 6, 15, or 22 lbs. ; in blocks of 7 or 10 lbs. Sold according to desired weight. The 45% is presented under the name Ski Queen, the 30% under the name Norse Star.

How to enjoy it : With a dry white wine, a light red, a rosé, or an apéritif wine.

A Country Recipe for Cheese

To serve 4 persons :

½ lb. of Nökkel in thick slices
4 eggs
½ pint of milk
8 to 10 slices of white bread
2 oz. of butter
Chives
1 pinch of salt
1 pinch of pepper

Mix the eggs and the milk. Add salt and pepper.

Butter the slices of bread, cover each one with a slice of Nökkel and place them in an oven dish.

Pour the egg-milk mixture over them and cook at 345° F. for about 20 minutes.

Sprinkle with chives just before serving.

REMARKS :

Norbo

Uses : Desserts, sandwiches, toast, hors-d'œuvres, as a condiment.

Origin : Norway.

Characteristics : Made from cow's milk. Fat (45%). Mild, delicate flavor. Creamy yellow crust covered with yellow or red wax. Rich, yellow paste, with small holes scattered throughout.

Related cheese : Gouda.

Appearance : In a block without a crust and in a wheel of 9 lbs. and in a miniature wheel.

How to enjoy it : With a Beaujolais, with a dry white Rhine or Moselle wine, or with beer.

Cheese and Celery Soufflé

To serve 4 to 6 people :

7 oz. of Norbo
2 tbsp. of grated cheese
2½ oz. of diced celery
3 eggs
2 oz. of diced bacon
7 liquid ounces of milk
½ pint of vegetable bouillon
3 tbsp. of butter
4 tbsp. of flour
¾ tsp. of salt

Once the celery has been cooked (about 10 minutes), mix together the flour and the butter with the milk and the vegetable bouillon.

Fry the bacon lightly in a frying pan and mix it with the egg yolks, the salt, the Norbo (diced) and the celery.

Beat the egg whites until stiff and mix all the ingredients in a well-greased oven dish.

Sprinkle with grated cheese and cook for 45 minutes at 390° F.

REMARKS :

Norvegia

Uses : Desserts, sandwiches, hors-d'œuvres, as a condiment, sauces for fish and for vegetables.

Origin : Norway.

Characteristics : Made from cow's milk. Fat (45%). Mild aromatic flavor. No crust. The pale yellow paste is semi-soft, rich, and slightly porous.

Related cheese : Samsoe.

Appearance : Comes in blocks of 7 and 10 lbs.

How to enjoy it : With a dry white wine (Rhine or Moselle), or a light red.

Norvegia with Bacon

Slice some Norvegia in tiny strips and roll them in thin slices of bacon.

Fix with toothpicks and season lightly with paprika.

Broil while turning the bacon rolls until the bacon becomes crispy and the cheese begins to melt.

Serve with rusks or crackers and a glass of beer.

Norvegia Cauliflower au Gratin

To serve four people :

One medium-size cauliflower
5 oz. of grated Norvegia
2 oz. of cooked ham
1 pint of milk
3 tbsp. of butter
4 tbsp. of flour
½ tsp. of salt
Chives (or 1 small, finely chopped onion)

Boil the cauliflower in salted water until it is tender.

Drain and place in an oven casserole dish.

Prepare a thick white sauce with the butter, the flour and the milk.

Add salt and then add the grated Norvegia.

Pour this sauce over the cauliflower and garnish with small pieces of ham and finely-chopped chives (or onion).

Brown in the oven and serve with baked potatoes.

REMARKS :

Oka

Uses : Desserts, snacks (with crackers or fruit).

Origin : Named after the village of Oka (Quebec), situated not far from the Abbey where it is made by the Trappist Fathers.

Characteristics : Extra-fat (48%). Mild, rich flavor. Natural crust. The paste is semi-soft, smooth, and juicy if the cheese is at room temperature. It is light yellow in color when made in the summer (the cattle being in pasture) ; white in winter. Made entirely by hand, it is only the craftsmanship of its manufacture which differentiates it from Port-Salut, which is prepared mechanically.

Related cheeses : Port-Salut, Saint-Paulin, Anfrom.

Appearance : Comes in small wheels of 5, 14, and 18 oz.

How to choose it : The crust must be smooth and healthy-looking, the paste both firm and tender.

Beware of a crust that is wrinkled, of a paste that is either dry or runny.

How to enjoy it : With a Beaujolais, a Corton, a Muscadet.

Historical background : Made for the first time in Canada by a French monk from the Abbey of Port-du-Salut (Entrammes, France).

REMARKS :

Parmesan (or Parmigiano-Reggiano or Grana)

Uses : Diverse. Desserts, and especially cooking (grated Parmesan on spaghetti, vegetables, in stews).

Origin : Italy (Province of Parma). Guaranteed by a label imprinted on the crust. There is also a Canadian-made Parmesan.

Characteristics : Made from cow's milk. Semi-fat (32%). Strong, spicy flavor. The crust is brushed, washed, and oiled. The paste is very hard, pressed and cooked, and melts in the mouth. Because of its granular nature, it is also called Grana.

Related cheeses : All Granas of other origins, Sbrinz.

Appearance : Comes in a convex-sided wheel of 65 lbs. on the average. It is sold according to desired weight, in prepared portions (weight variable) and in grated form (bags of 15 lbs., 8 oz. and 4 oz.).

How to choose it : Gives off a very faint odor. The dark brown crust must be smooth and very regular ; the paste fine, granular and of a good straw color.
Beware of a paste that is fissured, too granular, or rancid.

How to enjoy it : With a good red wine, a Lambrusco, and Asti Spumante.

Historical background : Already known in the Xth century. Introduced into France after the Italian wars (1496).

Cheese Polenta

To serve six people :

*14 oz. of corn semolina
1½ oz. of grated Parmesan
3½ oz. of butter*

Nutmeg
Oil

In a large pot, boil 2 quarts of slightly salted water and 1 pint in another, smaller pot.

Pour 14 oz. of corn semolina into the large pot and let it thicken by cooking while stirring continuously.

If the semolina becomes too thick, add boiling water from the reserve in the small pot.

When fully cooked, add 1½ oz. of grated Parmesan, 3½ oz. of butter, and a bit of nutmeg.

Serve hot as a thick soup or turn out onto a tray, spread to a thickness of ⅓ of an inch and allow to cool.

Once cut into slices, brown the Polenta in equal parts of oil and butter.

REMARKS :

Parmesan (Canadian)

Uses : Desserts, snacks, and especially in cooking in grated form (spaghetti, stews, vegetables).

Type : Italian.

Characteristics : Semi-fat. Strong, sharp flavor. Dark brown crust ; pale yellow paste that is very hard and granular.

Appearance : Comes in slices and grated : boxes of 8 oz. or bags of various weights.

How to enjoy it : With a good red wine or an Asti Spumante.

Parmesan Croquettes

For 25 croquettes :

10½ oz. of grated Parmesan
3 eggs
Flour
Breadcrumbs
Salt and pepper

Mix the Parmesan, salt, and pepper with the beaten egg whites.

Shape small balls and dip them successively in the flour, the egg yolks, and the breadcrumbs.

Fry in boiling oil until the croquettes are browned. Serve hot.

Parmesan Salad

Add some grated Parmesan to a salad consisting of the following : cabbage, lettuce, carrots, celery, and green onions. Season with vinaigrette dressing or with mayonnaise.

REMARKS :

Pecorino Romano

Uses : Desserts (when it is young). Old and grated : as a condiment for spaghetti, vegetables, stews.

Origin : Italy (Rome Province). There are also Romanos of Canadian and Dutch manufacture.

Characteristics : Made from ewe's milk. Semi-fat (32%). A very strong, sharp and peppery flavor, characteristic of ewe's milk cheese. Natural crust that is brushed, oiled with olive oil and sometimes colored with ochre. The paste is very hard, pressed, and cooked.

Appearance : Comes in a flat wheel of 13 to 50 lbs. and more. Sold by desired weight and in prepared portions. Process Dutch Romano comes in packages of 8 oz.

How to choose it : Gives off a faint smoky odor. The crust is white, yellow ochre, or greenish black ; the paste, white or light straw yellow, is very homogeneous and hard.
Beware of a paste that is too granular. The cheese will be too sharp, even though this is looked for by certain Romano fans.

How to enjoy it : With a Chianti or a Valpolicella.

Historical background : Already well-known in ancient Rome.

REMARKS :

Petit-Suisse

Uses : Handy for desserts (by itself or with fresh fruit), canapés, and some recipes.

Origin : France. Takes its name from the nationality of cattleman Charles Gervais. Around 1850, after immigrating to Paris, he advised the cheese-maker for whom he worked to add fresh cream to cream cheese.

Characteristics : Made from enriched cow's milk. Double-cream or triple-cream (60 to 75%). Extra-mild flavor. No

135

crust. The paste is white, soft, and of a creamy mildness, neither salted nor aged. By its very nature, it is not a cheese for export and its consumption cannot be other than local. There is also a Petit-Suisse made in Canada.

Appearance : Small cylinders in a 6-portion box (6 oz.). Comes both natural and with strawberries.

How to choose it : The only thing to look for is extreme freshness.

How to enjoy it : Wine is not necessary but it goes well with a red Bordeaux (St-Estèphe) or with beer.

Strawberry Mousse

Prepare a mousse with 4 Petit-Suisses, 7 oz. of fresh cream and 2¾ oz. of icing sugar.

Add 2 stiffly-beaten egg whites.

Blend into the mousse 8 or 9 oz. of strawberry halves and decorate with 8 whole strawberries.

REMARKS :

Picodon

Uses : Desserts, snacks.

Origin : France (Dauphiné). Gets its name from its sharp flavor.

Characteristics : Made from goat's milk. Fat (45%). A sharp flavor, but not excessively so. Natural crust. A soft paste steeped in white wine.

Appearance : Comes in a small irregular circle weighing 3 oz.

How to choose it : Gives off an odor of alcoholic fermentation. The crust is either golden or reddish in color. The paste must be firm but not hard.

Beware of a paste that is brittle or crumbly ; also of excessive fermentation (though some people prefer it that way).

How to enjoy it : With a white or red wine (Côtes-du-Rhône), a Meursault, a Hermitage.

REMARKS :

Pizza Cheese

Uses : Desserts, snacks, main dishes (baked rice, vegetables, etc.).

Type : Italian.

Characteristics : Made from milk that has been partially skimmed to 1.7%, 2%, or 3.2%. It is a mild cheese that is straw yellow in color. The paste is very compact and harder that that of Canadian Cheddar.

Appearance : Comes in a 5-lb. block, (sold in pizzerias).

REMARKS :

Pont-l'Évêque

Uses : Quite handy for desserts.

Origin : France. Named after the small town of Pont-l'Évêque in Normandy.

Characteristics : Made from cow's milk. Extra-fat (45 to 50%). Pronounced flavor. Washed crust. Soft paste that is neither pressed nor cooked.

Related cheese : Livarot.

Appearance : Comes in a square 12 oz. box.

How to choose it : The odor should be pleasant ; the crust golden yellow and very smooth ; the paste homogeneous, rich and at the same time both firm and flexible.

Beware of an odor of stables ; of a crust that is hard or greyish ; of a paste that is granular. A good Pont-l'Évêque should not be runny.

How to enjoy it : With a white Burgundy, a red Bordeaux, an Alsatian wine, or a bottled cider.

Historical background : Already known in the XIIIth century under the name of Angelot. The poet Guillaume de Lorris (circa 1235) mentions it in the first part of his *Romance of the Rose.*

REMARKS :

Port-Salut

Uses : Handy for desserts, toast, croque-madame.

Origin : France. Named after the Abbey of Port-du-Salut, in Entrammes (Maine).

Made to the end of the XIXth century by the Trappist Fathers who at that time sold their recipe and their trademark. More commonly known today by the name Saint-Paulin. (See listing.)

Appearance : Comes in a 4-lb. wheel and in a Baby Port-Salut that weighs 8 oz.

REMARKS :

Process Cheese

Uses : Desserts, sandwiches, canapés, cooking (sauces, salads, main dishes).

Characteristics : The paste is soft and smooth, and orange in color. The flavor varies from mild to sharp. This is a cheese that is ground, melted, pasteurized and mixed, prepared with Cheddar, cream cheese, Swiss or any other cheese, either alone or in combination. It can be moistened, and can have solid particles of milk, a coagulant, a preservative as well as various seasonings such as relish added to it. The finished product is poured into moulds, containers, or is wrapped.

There is also a lean process cheese, made from skim milk, which has only ⅓ of the fat content of a cheese made from whole milk. Finally, cheese spread is a soft process cheese, that is easy to spread, and which has the same water and fat content as another with a firm paste. Cheese spread is available with various seasonings, such as " Cheez Whiz " (with pimento), " Squeez-a-Snack " (smoked or with Mexican pimento), etc.

Appearance : Diverse.

REMARKS:

Process Cream Cheese

Uses : Desserts, with fruit, as a spread, in salad dressing, tarts, cheesecake.

Characteristics : Semi-fat (30.5%). Mild, slightly acid and in several flavors, this is a white, unaged cheese, that is soft and creamy. It is made by using 9% milk or a mixture of milk and cream to which is added either a lactic fermenting agent, or rennin, or both. The curd, once drained, provides a cheese with a fat content of 30.5%. It is sold natural, seasoned (pimento, relish, pineapple, etc.) or mixed with another cheese (Emmenthal, Camembert, etc.). Its very soft texture makes it an excellent cheese for spreading. One can also season it to one's own taste (sugar, salt or pepper), or add herbs, etc.

Appearance : Generally comes in foil-wrapped packages of 4 or 8 oz. depending on the product.

Lemon Tarts

For 18 tarts :

8 oz. of softened cream cheese
18 cooked tart shells of 2 inches in diameter
3 egg yolks
3 egg whites
½ cup of sugar

6 tbsp. of sugar
¼ cup of lemon juice
1 tbsp. of grated lemon rind
Salt

Beat the egg yolks with the ½ cup of sugar and a pinch of salt.

Add the lemon juice and rind. Cook in a double-boiler, while stirring, until the mixture is thick and smooth.

Allow to cool, gradually add the cream cheese and pour into the tart shells.

Whip the egg whites (with a pinch of salt) so that they become firm but not dry, add the 6 tbsp. of sugar one at a time while continuing to beat until the meringue is firm and lustrous.

Use it to garnish the tarts and then brown them at 425°F. for 3 to 5 minutes. Let cool before serving.

Clam Dip

4 oz. of cream cheese
1 tin (10 oz.) of clams, drained and finely chopped
1 tbsp. of clam juice
1 tbsp. of lemon juice
A few drops of hot sauce
Salt and pepper

Beat the cheese until a light consistency is obtained. Add all the ingredients and mix well.

POIDS NET
113 g
PRODUCT OF DENMARK

CONTROL
NO. 2244

NET WEIGHT
4 OZ.
IMPORTE DU DANEMARK

PROCESS CREAM CHEESE SPREAD · FROMAGE A LA CREME FONDU.A TARTINER

Cheese and Cucumber Garnish

For approximately 1 cup of garnishing :

4 oz. of cream cheese
2 tbsp. of mayonnaise
½ cup of finely diced cucumbers
1 tbsp. of chopped onions
Salt and pepper

Mix the cheese and the mayonnaise thoroughly until smooth and creamy and then add the rest of the ingredients.

Cheese and Honey Sauce

For approximately ⅔ of a cup of sauce :

4 oz. of cream cheese
2 tbsp. of liquid honey
1 tbsp. of lemon juice

Mix the cheese, honey, and lemon, beat until smooth, and serve with a fruit salad.

REMARKS :

143

Provolone

Uses: Quite handy. Desserts. When old and hard, it can be grated and used as a seasoning for cooking.

Origin: Italy (Compania). Takes its name from the Campanian dialect word " prova " (spherically-shaped cheese). There are also Canadian, Dutch, and American-made Provolones.

Characteristics : Made from cow's milk. Fat (44%). Its flavor is delicate and mild, becoming strong and even very strong (bitter, sharp, smoky-tasting) with age. Natural, smooth crust. The paste is strained, hard, uncooked.

Appearance : Comes in the shape of a melon or a salami (5, 10, 25, and 50 lbs.) Sold by desired weight.

How to choose it: Gives off a mild, lactic odor. The golden yellow or brown crust should be smooth, thin and shiny; the paste should be creamy white or straw colored, compact, soft, and flexible.

Beware of a paste that has holes due to interior fermentation.

How to enjoy it: With a Beaujolais or a Broglio.

REMARKS :

Provolone (Canadian)

Uses: Soft: snacks, sandwiches, main dishes. Hard: grated for cooking.

Type: Italian.

Characteristics: Extra-fat (48%). The flavor is smoky, bitter and spicy and becomes more and more accentuated with age. Natural, dark-brown crust; pale yellow paste that is firm and smooth.

Appearance: Comes in salami shapes of 10, 25, and 50 lbs. Sold by desired weight.

How to enjoy it: With a dry white, red or rosé wine.

REMARKS:

Puck

Uses: Desserts, snacks, sandwiches.

Characteristics: Extra-fat (48%). This is a cheese of the Saint-Paulin type, but with a firmer texture and a slightly less-pronounced flavor.

Appearance: Comes in a small 6 oz. wheel reminiscent of the famous hockey puck dear to the hearts of all sports fans.

Historical background: Made in Dunham, Quebec.

REMARKS:

Pyramid (or Valençay)

Uses: Quite handy for desserts.

Origin : France (Touraine). Named after the small town of Valençay.

Characteristics: Made from goat's milk. Fat (45%). Mild flavor. Downy crust. The paste is soft, uncooked, and lightly salted.

Related Cheeses : All goat's milk cheeses. There are more than sixty different varieties.

Appearance: Comes in a small, truncated pyramid of 6 or 7 oz.

How to choose it: Gives off an odor of goats and of mould. The crust should be white, without too much of a greyish tinge. The paste should be firm but flexible. Be careful of a paste that is granular or too hard. The cheese risks being too salty.

How to enjoy it: With a Sancerre, a Pouilly, a Moulin-à-Vent. With any dry white wine or light red wine.

REMARKS :

Reblochon

Uses: Desserts.

Origin: France (Savoy). Takes its name from the verb "reblocher" which means "to milk cows a second time" (Savoy dialect).

Characteristics: Made from the milk of hill cattle. Extra-fat (50%). A nutty flavor that is mild and creamy. Washed crust. A paste that is soft, lightly salted, and uncooked.

Related cheeses : Port-Salut, Saint-Paulin, Oka.

Appearance : Comes in a round box weighing 16 oz. or 8 oz. under the name of Reblochonnet.

How to choose it: Gives off a faint, musty odor. The crust, which is a flat pinkish-yellow color, should be healthy-looking and smooth; the paste should be tender and very supple.

Beware of a crust that is hard or a paste that is granular. The cheese will probably be bitter.

How to enjoy it: With a white Burgundy, an Alsatian wine, or a Moulin-à-Vent.

Historical background: This is a very old cheese. Four or five hundred years ago — history does not tell us if the practice still exists today — the herdsmen used to poach milk by remilking the animals after the "foreman" had left. This is undoubtly why this cheese, which they made for their personal use, remained unknown to gourmets for so long.

REMARKS:

Regidiet

A lean diet cheese (0%).
Gournay type.

Lightly-salted and spiced with parsley.
Can be kept for two to three months.
Comes in a 5 oz. portion in a small blue, yellow and white cardboard container.

REMARKS:

Ricotta Fresca

Uses: Used in the same way as cottage cheese. Desserts and snacks (sweetened or salted according to taste), main dishes, lasagna, spaghetti, pastas, Italian cakes. Excellent with fruit or jam.

Type: Italian.

Characteristics: Made with whole milk or with a mixture of whole milk and whey. This is a fresh cheese that is soft and moist, granular and with a white curd. The flavor is nutty, mild and sweet. Similar to a cottage cheese or a thick double-cream, but with a more flexible consistency.

Appearance: Comes in a 20 oz. box.

REMARKS:

Romano

Uses: Desserts when it is young. When old, it is mostly used grated for cooking (spaghetti, vegetables, stews).

Type: Italian.

Characteristics: Semi-fat. A light smoky odor and a flavor that is sharp and peppery. The crust is a greenish-black; the paste is creamy, very hard, and granular.

Appearance: Comes in a wheel.

How to enjoy it: With a Chianti or a Valpolicella.

REMARKS:

Roquefort (French Blue)

Uses: Very handy for desserts, canapés, toast, croque-monsieur, salad dressing.

Origin: France. Comes from the small town of Roquefort-sur-Soulzon (in Aquitaine).

Characteristics: Made from ewe's milk. Fat (45%). Pronounced ovine flavor, sometimes strong or even very strong. Natural crust. The paste is soft, sprinkled with interior mould, oily, rich in casein, and is marbled with green. Aged in the famous natural caves of the Cliff of Cambalou. This is a cheese that is nutritious, digestible, and very much appreciated.

Related cheese: Corsican Blue, which is also made from ewe's milk.

Appearance: Comes foil-wrapped with a red label. In wheels weighing 5 to 6 lbs. Sold in slices of 3 and 6 ounces.

How to choose it : Must give off a faint, but very definite, mouldy odor. The crust should be healthy-looking ; the paste firm, smooth, oily, and veined throughout.

Be careful of a cheese that is eroded around the edges, that is grey or too white, or that lacks marbling. It risks being sharp.

How to enjoy it: With a Chateauneuf-du-Pape, a Chambertin, a Hermitage, a Haut-Brion, or spirits.

How to keep it: Never under a cheese cover. In the shade and open to the air, at a normal temperature.

Historical background: Its reputation was already established in ancient Rome, and its fame has never lessened over the centuries. Pliny the Elder, who perished in the eruption of Vesuvius at Pompeii (79 A.D.), mentions it in his " Natural History ". Charlemagne was converted to Roquefort by a Spanish bishop who presented a whole case of it to him. Later, the popes who were in residence in Avignon received it as an annual tribute. Rabelais,

King Louis XV, and Casanova all paid homage to it. According to the latter, who must have known what he was talking about, it would seem that Roquefort has virtues other than those which are strictly gastronomical.

Eggs Stuffed with Roquefort

To make 12 eggs:

12 hard-boiled eggs
1 oz. of Petit-Suisse
20 finely-chopped olives
¾ oz. of very finely-minced bacon
⅓ oz. of Double-Crème

Take the hard-boiled eggs, cut them in half, and remove the yolks.
Make a paste of all the ingredients, including the yolks, and use it to replace the yolks.

Serve with HP sauce.

REMARKS:

Saint-Benoit

Uses: Desserts, snacks, cooking.

Origin: The Benedictine Monastery of Saint-Benoit-du-Lac, (Quebec). There is also a Saint-Benoit made in France.

Characteristics: Extra-fat (48%). It is of the same type as a Swiss Gruyère, but the paste is less firm. It has numerous small holes.

Appearance : Comes in wheels of 11 to 14 lbs. ; also in 8 oz. portions.

REMARKS:

Saint-Marcellin (or Tomme de Saint-Marcellin)

Uses: Handy for desserts.

Origin: France (Dauphiné). Comes from Saint-Marcellin, a small town not far from Grenoble.

Characteristics: Used to be made solely with goat's milk. Today, it is made with cow's milk, or with a mixture of the two. Extra-fat (50%). Mild flavor. Natural crust. The paste is soft, lightly salted, and uncooked.

Related cheese: Tomme de Roman.

Appearance: Comes in a small, paper-wrapped disc that weighs 3 oz..

How to choose it: Gives off a faint lactic odor. The grey-blue crust should be delicate; the paste flexible and uniform.

Beward of a paste that is not uniform, granular, or too salty.

How to enjoy it: With a light Beaujolais, a Moulin-à-Vent, a Bourgueil, a Hermitage.

Historical background: Very old. Discovered and enjoyed by Louis XI of France as the result of a dangerous bear hunt in Vercors. He was rescued by two woodcutters, who restored him with the local cheese. Imprudently having promised each of them a reward of 10,000 écus,

151

the king judged that it was more economical to raise both of them to the nobility in 1447.

REMARKS:

Sainte-Maure

Uses: Good for desserts and snacks.

Origin: France (Touraine). Named after the small town of Sainte-Maure-en-Touraine, a central cheese market in the area.

Characteristics: Made from goat's milk and prepared the same way as Camembert. Fat (45%). Mild flavor. Natural crust. The paste is soft, lightly salted, and uncooked.

Appearance: Comes in cylinders of 5, and 6 to 7 oz.

How to choose it: Gives off a rather pronounced odor of goats. The crust should be a bluish-white, marbled with orangey-yellow; the paste should be firm and rich.

Beware of a paste that is too hard and granular. The cheese risks being too salty. A runny cheese is also to be avoided.

Hgw to enjoy it: With a dry Vouvray, a Chinon, a Bourgueil, a Muscadet.

REMARKS:

Saint-Nectaire

Uses: Desserts, toasted snacks.

Origin: France (Auvergne). Named for Saint-Nectaire, the principal center of production.

Characteristics: Made from the milk of hill cattle. Fat (45%). Mild, very pleasant flavor. Natural, downy crust. The paste is semi-soft, uncooked, and very rich.

Appearance: Comes in a wheel that weighs about 3 lbs.. Sold according to desired weight.

How to choose it : Gives off an odor of mushrooms. Greyish or slightly violet, the crust is sometimes tinged with yellow and red moulds. The paste should be supple without being soft.

How to enjoy it: With a Tavel, Hermitage, Chinon, Bouzy.

REMARKS:

Saint-Paulin

Uses: Good for desserts, canapés, croque-madame.

Origin: France. Manufactured according to the recipe of the Trappist Fathers of the Abbey of Port-du-Salut, it is obviously named after Saint-Paulin, the bishop of Nole in the VIth century. There are also Canadian and Danish-made Saint-Paulins.

Characteristics: Made from cow's milk. Extra-fat (45 to

50%). Mild, rich flavor. Washed crust. The paste is semi-soft, pressed, and slightly cooked.

Related cheeses: Port-Salut, Bonbel, Anfrom, Oka, etc.

Appearance: Comes in a wheel of 3½ lbs.; in a small, transparently wrapped wheel of 7 oz.; in 6 oz. slices.

How to choose it: Gives off a faint odor of fermented milk. The crust is smooth, waxed, of an attractive reddish-orange color; the paste is a creamy yellow, tender, smooth, and mild.

Beware of a fermented crust, of a dry or granular paste, or one in which the color is not uniform throughout. The cheese could easily be sharp.

How to enjoy it: With a Beaujolais, a Muscadet, an Anjou, a Corton.

REMARKS:

Saint-Paulin (Canadian)

Uses: Desserts, snacks, canapés, croque-madame.

Characteristics: Extra-fat (48 to 50%). Mild flavor, but more pronounced than that of the imported Saint-Paulin. The washed crust is a yellow orange. The paste is smooth, pressed, semi-soft, and yellowish-white in color.

Appearance: Depending on the make: in a 4 or 5 lb. wheel, in points of 6 or 8 oz.

How to enjoy it: With a red, white, or sparkling wine.

Samsoe

Uses: Good for desserts, snacks.

Origin: Denmark.

Characteristics: Made from whole milk. Fat (45%). Mild, nutty flavor, more or less pronounced, depending on the degree of aging. Colored crust. The paste is semi-soft, pressed, uncooked, and pierced with openings.

Related Danish Cheeses: Elbo, red crust, pear-shaped. Tybo, red crust, in a block of 5 lbs.
Molbo, red crust, in a ball.
Fynbo, yellow crust, in a wheel.
Danbo, yellow crust, in a square.

Appearance: Comes in a wheel or a block weighing 30 or 10 lbs. Sold by desired weight. Also available in a prepared portion (7 oz.).

How to enjoy it: With a Médoc, a Graves, a Pomerol, a Beaujolais.

Sbrinz

Uses: Quite handy. Rarely used as a dessert, but rather in cooking (grated).

Origin: Switzerland (Uri, Schwyz, and Unterwald Cantons).

Characteristics: Made from cow's milk. Fat (45%). Full-bodied, very pronounced flavor. The crust is smooth, brushed, and oiled. The paste is pressed and cooked. Very digestible, it is good for those with delicate stomachs. Keeps for a fairly long period of time.

Related cheeses: Parmesan, Reggiano, Italian Grana.

Appearance: Comes in wheels of 70 to 80 lbs. Sold according to desired weight. Also sold in grated form.

How to choose it: Gives off a faint rancid odor. The crust is dark yellow. The paste is yellow, compact, hard, and brittle.

Be careful of a paste that is granular and crumbly.

Historical background: Known in ancient Rome. Mentioned by Pliny, the Roman historian, under the name of "Caesus Helvetius".

REMARKS :

Scamorza

Uses: Desserts (with fruit), hors d'oeuvres, and cooking.
Type: Italian.

Characteristics: Made from partially skimmed milk (1 or 2%) to which a lactic fermenting agent and rennin are added. It is then worked in hot water to give it its spherical shape. The paste is an ivory color which darkens with age; it is then that it is at its best. Can be kept for two to three months.

Related cheeses: Caciocavallo, Provolone.

Appearance: Comes in a small ball of 10 or 12 oz. that has a point to it which permits hanging the cheese so that it will dry out.

Scamorza Fried Eggs

Brown slices of Scamorza in a frying pan and then fry the eggs on top of them.

REMARKS:

Skimmy Cheese

Uses : A diet cheese used for spreading.

Characteristics : Lean (15%). Made from partially skimmed milk.

Appearance : Comes in a 4 lb. wheel. Sold by desired weight.

REMARKS :

Sour Cream

Uses : Good with fruit as a dessert, in pastry, for cooking (cake, steaks, baked potatoes, etc.).

Characteristics : Lean (18%). Made from acidified 18% milk and treated with a lactic fermenting agent and rennin to give it more consistency. The addition of a preservative gives it a life span of three weeks.

REMARKS :

Stilton (or Blue Stilton)

Uses: Desserts, toast, canapés.

Origin: England (Leicestershire). Takes its name from the town of Stilton wher it was originally sold. There is also a Norwegian Stilton.

Characteristics: Made from cow's milk. Extra-fat (55%). Strong, pleasant flavor. Natural brushed crust. Soft paste with interior mould.

Related cheeses: All blue cheeses.

Appearance: Comes in foil-wrapped wheels of 5 or 15 lbs. in earthenware pots of 1 lb. or 8 oz. ; in a mini-pot (4 oz.) ; in plastic cups (4 and 8 oz.) ; in plastic-wrapped points of various weights.

How to choose it: Gives off quite a pronounced mouldy smell. The grey crust should be healthy-looking and regular ; the paste should be firm, a bit flexible, and well-marbled.

Be careful of a paste that is granular. It could be bitter or too sharp.

How to enjoy it: With a Chambertin, a Chateauneuf-du-Pape.

Toast or Cañapés

Steep the Stilton in sherry, Madeira, or port. It will then be excellent for toast or canapés. Accompany it with the same wine as that in which it was steeped.

REMARKS:

Suprême (or Fin-de-Siècle)

Uses : Desserts.

Origin : France (Bray). Takes its name from the era of its creation (1890).

Characteristics : Made from enriched milk. Double-cream (72%). Mild flavor. Downy crust. Soft paste.

Related cheeses : Brillat-Savarin, Excelsior, Parfait.

Appearance : Small flat, irregular discs of 6 oz. or of 4 oz. under the name of Suprême Bébé.

How to choose it : Gives off a faint odor of cream and mushrooms. The crust should be downy, but not excessively so. The paste should be firm and compact, without elasticity.

Swiss Cheese (Emmenthal)

Uses: Desserts, sandwiches, fondues, salads, sauces.

Type: Swiss.

Characteristics: Extra-fat (48%). Mild, sweet, nutty flavor. The golden yellow crust is hard and dry. The paste is smooth and very firm, and pierced with large holes.

There is also a Process Swiss manufactured that has the same taste. Its creamy yellow paste is soft and smooth, without a single hole.

How to enjoy it: With a red, white, or sparkling white wine, or with beer.

Quiche Lorraine

For 6 persons:

1 9-in. pie crust
1 cup of grated Swiss cheese
6 slices of fried bacon, crumbled
3 beaten eggs
1¼ cups of table cream
¼ cup of milk
1 tbsp. of butter
Salt, pepper, cayenne, and nutmeg

Mix the Swiss cheese and the bacon and distribute evenly over the bottom of the pie shell.

Add knobs of butter (1 tbsp. in all).

Mix the beaten eggs, cream, milk, and spices and pour over the cheese.

Brown at 375°F. for about 35 to 40 minutes.

Swiss Fondue

See recipe on page 113.

Instead of using a mixture of Gruyère and Emmenthal, use 2 cups of grated Swiss cheese.

Just before serving, a bit of kirsch can be added.

REMARKS :

Tilsit

Uses : Versatile. Desserts, snacks, sandwiches, canapés.

Origin : Switzerland (Saint Gall and Thurgovia Cantons). There are also Tilsits of Canadian, Norwegian, and Finnish (Krewi) manufacture.

Characteristics : Made from cow's milk. Fat (45%). Pronounced fruity flavor, slightly bitter and sharp. The crust is brushed and greased. The paste is pressed, uncooked.

Related cheeses : Toupin, Krewi.

Appearance : Comes in a slightly convex-sided flat wheel of 9 to 11 lbs. Sold according to desired weight.

How to choose it : Gives off a strong musty odor. The red ochre crust must be regular and even ; the yellowish paste must be semi-firm, plastic but not soft, and pierced with a number of small holes.
Be careful of a granular paste or of insufficient aging.

How to enjoy it : With a light red wine or with beer.

Historical background : Undoubtedly it originally came from East Prussia and was introduced into Switzerland in the XVIIIth century.

Tilsit Salad

Cover the bottom of a salad bowl with a bed of lettuce leaves.

Dice some Tilsit and place it on the leaves.

Garnish with pitted olives and rolled anchovies.

Just before serving, pour on a salad dressing (oil and lemon juice) seasoned with capers and freshly-ground pepper.

REMARKS :

Tilsit (Canadian)

Uses : Desserts, sandwiches, canapés. When old, it is used as a condiment.

Type : Swiss.

Characteristics : Extra-fat (48%). Slightly sharp flavor. Red ochre crust ; the yellowish paste is semi-soft, plastic in texture, and pierced with a number of small holes.

How to enjoy it : With a light red wine or with beer.

REMARKS :

Tomme de Savoie

Uses : Desserts, snacks, toast.

Origin : France (Savoy).

Characteristics : Made from cow's milk, and occasionally from goat's milk, but this is indicated on the label (Tomme de Chèvre). Lean or fat (20 to 40%). Pronounced flavor. Natural brushed crust. The paste is pressed, uncooked, and slowly aged in grape skins.

Appearance : In wheels of 3 to 4 lbs. Sold in points of 4 oz.

How to choose it : Gives off a very pronounced aroma due to its special aging. The crust must be regular, and tinged with yellow, red, and grey. The yellowish paste should be flexible.

Beware of a wrinkled crust ; of a granular paste that is pink and spotted with brown. The cheese could be bitter.

How to enjoy it : With a Mondeuse, an Arbin, a Fleurie.

REMARKS :

Vacherin du Jura

Uses : Desserts.

Origin : France (Franche-Comté).

Characteristics : Made from cow's milk. Fat (45%). Mild, creamy, resinous flavor. Washed crust. The paste is soft, slightly pressed, and uncooked.

Appearance : Comes in wheels of 5 to 6 lbs., encircled with pine bark. Sold according to desired weight.

How to choose it : Gives off a faint odor of resin and lactic fermentation. The crust should be smooth, shiny, and pinkish. The paste should be tender and rich.

Beware of a crust that is rough, wrinkled, hardened, or mouldy ; of a paste that is too hard. The cheese risks being bitter.

How to enjoy it : With a Montmélian, a Beaujolais, a Crépy.

REMARKS :

Wensleydale

Origin : England.

Characteristics : Made from cow's milk. Light yellow in color. It has a very delicate flavor with an aftertaste of honey.

Appearance : Comes in wheels of approximately 10 lbs., wrapped in plastic. Also in a 1 lb. minicheese.

REMARKS :

Winchee

Uses : Desserts, snacks, appetizers, cocktail hors-d'œuvres.

Characteristics : Fat (40%). Creamy marbled paste, made by mixing two Cheddars (mild and strong) with powdered skim milk and flavored with red and white wine. Can be kept for one or two months.

Composition : Fromage cheddar vieilli, poudre de petit-lait, poudre de lait écrémé, vin, beurre, gomme végétale, sorbate de potassium, colorants.
Ingredients : Aged cheddar cheese, whey powder, skim-milk powder, wine, butter, vegetable gum, potassium sorbate, colours.

CONSERVER AU FROID

KEEP REFRIGERATED

POIDS NET : 5 LB.

WINCHEE

NET WEIGHT : 5 LB.

FAIT AU CANADA

MADE IN CANADA

Aromatisé au Vin - Flavored with Wine

PRODUITS ALIMENTAIRES ANCO FOOD PRODUCTS INC.

MONTREAL, OTTAWA, QUEBEC, TORONTO, VANCOUVER, CANADA

Related cheese : Nippican, a Canadian cheese that is aged in wine and presented in wheels of 5 lbs. and 10 oz.

Appearance : Comes in a 5 lb. wheel and is sold according to desired weight.

Historical background : Manufactured only since 1970. One of the favorite cheeses of English Canada.

REMARKS :

Yogurt

Uses : Lunches, desserts, snacks.

Origin : Bulgaria. Takes its name from the Bulgarian word for naturally coagulated milk.

Characteristics : Made from cow's milk and obtained by allowing a lactic fermenting agent to act on boiled milk. Its nature requires local production. The flavor is fresh and a bit acidic.

Appearance : Naturally flavored (coffee, vanilla) or mixed with various fruit-based preparations (strawberries, raspberries, pineapple, etc.). Comes in pots of 6, 16, or 32 liquid ounces.

How to choose it : Look for freshness. The date limit for consumption is indicated on the container.

To make your own delicious Yogurt

All that's needed is :

1 quart of homogenized whole milk
1 small container of commercial yogurt (natural)

A kitchen thermometer and a receptacle that can be hermetically sealed (preferably plastic as it will hold the heat better).

In a pot, boil the milk until it no longer " rises ", which should take about 3 minutes.
Each time the milk rises, remove the pot from the heat for an instant, so that it will not boil over.

Allow to cool to 115° F. and add two full tablespoons of yogurt.

Pour the mixture into the plastic receptacle, close tightly, and allow to stand for 3 to 4 hours away from both heat and light (for example, in the empty oven, if none of the stove burners are in use).

REMARKS :

New York is a gothic Roquefort ! .....

Salvador Dali

166

Conversion Tables

Editor's note

As weights and measures have been expressed in Anglo-Saxon units avoirdupois, the measures in general use throughtout North America, we have prepared the following conversion tables for your convenience.

Avoirdupois	METRIC SYSTEM	ANGLO-SAXON SYSTEM
	28 grams	1 ounce
	35 grams	1¼ ounce
	42,5 grams	1½ ounce
	50 grams	1¾ ounce
	100 grams	3½ ounces
	125 grams	4¼ ounces
	200 grams	7 ounces
	250 grams	9 ounces
	300 grams	10 ounces
	500 grams (1 livre) mét.	18 ounces

Powdered Products (flour, spices, coffee, etc.)	METRIC SYSTEM	ANGLO-SAXON SYSTEM
	3 grams	1 teaspoon
	9 grams	1 soup spoon
	50 grams	4 soup spoons
	125 grams	9 spoonful (¼ lb.)
	250 grams	18 spoonsful (½ lb.)
	500 grams	36 spoonsful (1 lb.)

Sugar	METRIC SYSTEM	ANGLO-SAXON SYSTEM
	5 grams	1 teaspoon
	15 grams	1 soup spoon
	50 grams	3 soup spoons
	125 grams	6½ soup spoons (¼ lb.)
	250 grams	13 soup spoons (½ lb.)
	500 grams	26 soup spoons (1 lb.)

Butter	METRIC SYSTEM	ANGLO-SAXON SYSTEM
	50 grams	2 soup spoons
	125 grams	4½ soup spoons (¼ lb.)
	250 grams	9 soup spoons (½ lb.)
	500 grams	18 soup spoons (1 lb.)

Liquids

METRIC SYSTEM	ANGLO-SAXON SYSTEM
60 drops	1 teaspoon
2 teaspoons	1 dessert spoon
2 dessert spoons	1 soup spoon
16 soup spoons	1 cup
½ centilitre	1 teaspoon
1 centilitre	2 teaspoons (⅓ ounce)
1½ centilitre	1 soup spoon
½ decilitre	3 soup spoons and 1 teaspoon
1 decilitre	6 soup spoons and 2 teaspoons
2 decilitres	13 soup spoons and 1 teaspoon
2¼ decilitres	15 soup spoons or 1 cup
2½ decilitres (¼ litre)	1 half-pint
3 decilitres	20 soup spoons
4 decilitres	26 soup spoons
4½ decilitres	30 soup spoons or 2 cups
¼ de litre	1 half-pint
½ litre	1 pint
1 litre	4½ cups or 1 quart and 3½ ounces
1⅛ litre	1 quart

Equivalents

1 coffee spoon	30 drops	2.5 cc.
1 teaspoon	2 coffee spoons or 60 drops	5 cc.
1 dessert spoon	2 teaspoons	10 cc.
1 tablespoon	3 teaspoons	
1 soup spoon	½ liquid ounce	15 cc.
2 tablespoons	1 liquid ounce	30 cc.
¼ cup	1 wine glass	2 ounces
1 pinch	⅛ teaspoon	
1 cubic centimetre	1 millilitre	1/30 ounce
1 decilitre		3.5 ounces
⅛ cup	2 tablespoons	30 cc.
¼ cup	4 tablespoons	60 cc.
½ cup	8 tablespoons	120 cc.
1 cup	{ 16 tablespoons / 8 ounces / ½ pint	240 cc.
2 cups	1 pint	0.560 litre
5 cups	1 quart	1 litre 14
1 ounce	2 tablespoons	30 cc.
2 ounces	4 tablespoons	60 cc.
4 ounces	8 tablespoons	120 cc.
8 ounces	16 tablespoons	240 cc.
16 ounces	1 pint	0.568 litre
40 ounces	1 quart	1 litre 14

Contents